vegan

in association with the Vegan Society vegan®

Tony Weston and Yvonne Bishop

hamlyn

First published in Great Britain in 2004 by
Hamlyn, a division of Octopus Publishing Group Ltd
2–4 Heron Quays, London E14 4JP

ISBN 0 600 60915 4

A CIP catalogue record for this book is available from the British Library

Printed and bound in China

10 9 8 7 6 5 4 3 2 1

Both metric and imperial measurements are given for the recipes. Use one set of
measures only, not a mixture of both.

Ovens should be preheated to the specified temperature. If using a fan-assisted
oven, follow the manufacturer's instructions for adjusting the time and temperature.
Grills should also be preheated.

Fresh herbs should be used unless otherwise stated. If unobtainable, use dried herbs
as an alternative but halve the quantities stated.

Pepper should be freshly ground unless otherwise specified.

A few recipes include nuts and nut derivatives. Anyone with a known nut allergy
must avoid these.

This book is registered with the Vegan Society. Nothing printed should be construed to
be Vegan Society policy unless so stated. Any views or opinions presented are solely
those of the authors and do not necessarily represent those of the Vegan Society.

The Vegan Society
Donald Watson House
7 Battle Road
St Leonards on Sea
East Sussex
TN37 7AA
United Kingdom
Telephone: 0845 4588244
Fax: 01424 717064

www.vegansociety.com

contents

introduction

Like many people, you're probably eating rather differently from the way you did as a child: less meat, more fruit and veg, lower fat, sugar and salt. Maybe you've even cut meat and fish out of your diet and are already vegetarian. Perhaps you're now wondering what else you can do to avoid animal products and contributing towards the wasteful use of the world's resources.

Wherever you currently stand in your food philosophy, this book is for you. Tony Weston, a vegan for many years, and Yvonne Bishop BSc Dip ION MBANT, a nutrition therapist, have compiled a selection of their favourite recipes and invite you to try a delicious cuisine that will almost certainly surprise you in its variety and taste. Banish thoughts of tired nut roasts and predictable vegetable stir-fries. Here you will find newly available ingredients, such as chlorella algae and quinoa, alongside old favourites, such as tofu and carob, to push the boundaries of vegan cuisine as never before. The authors gently dispel any misconceptions you might have that veganism involves tyrannical self-denial and prove that vegan food can be everything you want – delicious, attractive, healthy and full of choice.

Starting with a section of basic recipes that includes some of the staples essential to the vegan repertoire, the book is then divided into four main sections – breakfasts, light meals, main meals and desserts. As you'll quickly discover, the pleasures of good food without animal products are quite real and easily achievable. Imagine a day that starts with Chocolate Croissants or Creamy Mushrooms on Toast, moves on to a lunch of Asparagus Pancakes or Apricot, Beetroot and Cumin Soup, then finishes with Chestnut Cottage Pies or Arame Almond Risotto, followed by Banoffee and Quinoa Custard Pie or Date and Prune Brownies.

There are recipes for every occasion, from simple snacks to sophisticated dinner dishes, allowing for the fact that some days you have more time than others. You will also find quick fixes to hunger pangs, as well as our top ten sandwich ideas – all part of helping you to break the habit of skipping meals and relying on fast food and take-aways to fill the gaps.

Worried that vegan food might not supply enough nutrients to keep you healthy, energetic and alert? Just consult the section dealing with vitamins and minerals (see pages 8–10 to find out what you need and how a varied vegan diet can supply it. Any possible shortfalls are pointed out and ways of compensating are suggested).

Far from being difficult and extreme, veganism is easy, straightforward and delicious – a great way to achieve optimum health and a clearer conscience.

what is veganism?

The philosophy of veganism is far from new, and many religions teach a reverence for life and compassion for living things.

The Greek philosopher Pythagoras (c.569-c.475 BC) taught the virtue of eating without causing suffering; those who followed the vegetarianism he espoused were known as Pythagoreans. Some 2000 years later Leonardo da Vinci predicted, 'The time will come when men such as I will look upon the murder of animals as they now look on the murder of men.' Whatever your reasons for cutting animal products out of your life, it is a decision you will never regret.

The Vegan Society

Less than 100 years after the UK Vegetarian Society was formed in 1847, the ethics of consuming dairy products were being hotly debated. An attempt to establish a non-dairy group within the Vegetarian Society was rejected, so in 1944, a member named Donald Watson (b. 1910) was moved to act. He coined a new name for the non-dairy philosophy, announcing, '...vegan is the beginning and end of vegetarian'. The Vegan Society was founded in November 1944.

The Vegan Society is a charity bound by its constitution to educate, provide information and promote ways of living free from animal products for the benefit of people, animals and the environment. Veganism seeks 'to exclude all forms of exploitation of, and cruelty to, animals for food, clothing or any other purpose'. In brief, it makes no sense to exploit animals for food: everything we need for good health and happiness can be found without using animal-based products. There are now vegan societies in countries all over the world, numerous books have been published under its auspices, and the Vegan Society trademark of authenticity can be seen on thousands of products.

Suitable for...

Unlike many other food products, those labelled 'suitable for vegans' are actually suitable for nearly everyone. They meet the needs of those avoiding certain meats for religious reasons; of those cutting down on saturated fat; of those who suffer dietary intolerances; and, of course, of those who are vegetarian.

As manufacturers increasingly tap into the vegan market with its millions of adherents, so they add to the range of vegan products on offer. The variety is now so impressive – and so widely available – that shoppers of all dietary persuasions are as likely to buy vegan products as the non-vegan varieties, simply because they are delicious, versatile and nutritious.

The Animal Free Shopper, the Vegan Society's shopping guide, gets bigger and better with every edition; you can even buy vegan condoms, cameras and shoes. Vegans are a growing market and manufacturers take their needs very seriously.

Everybody's doing it

Increasing numbers of people are realizing the potential of veganism and recognizing that it has become easier and more delicious than ever to follow. Research shows that most of us would prefer to be kinder to people, animals and the environment, and would do so in our shopping habits if it were always possible to choose an ethically produced item over one that might, for example, use child labour. Veganism is the solution to pleasing everyone, to being inclusive rather than exclusive.

Even if you are vegan for only 50 per cent of the time, your actions combine with those of others to make a real difference to the planet. Don't view making the change as one big leap that requires 100 per cent commitment. Do as much as you feel comfortable with and everyone will reap the rewards.

are you getting enough?

A balanced vegan diet can provide all the nutrients needed for a healthy body; even B12 (essential to protect your nervous system and heart health), which is found mainly in meat and other animal products, can now be obtained from fortified foods or supplements. Just as important is to get the right balance of omega-6 fats (from grains) and omega-3 fats (from plants and seeds).

PROTEINS

Proteins are vital for growth and repair, and for regulating most body functions. They include enzymes (to help metabolism), hormones (to send chemical messages) and antibodies (to boost the immune system). Proteins are made in the body by different combinations of amino-acid building blocks.

Some plant foods, such as amaranth, buckwheat, quinoa and soya, have all the essential amino acids, so are often referred to as 'complete' proteins. However, complete proteins can also be made in the body as long as all the essential amino acids are obtained from the diet in a 48-hour period.

Examples of complete protein combinations include:
• Grains or nuts with legumes
• Rice or millet with vegetables
• Vegetables with mushrooms
• Vegetables with sesame seeds or Brazil nuts

Protein requirements depend on age and activity, and increase during pregnancy and lactation. The ideal average protein intake for an adult is about 20 per cent of the daily food intake. A varied vegan diet can easily provide this. Protein-rich foods include pulses (peas, lentils, beans and bean products, such as tofu and tempeh), pseudo-grains (amaranth, buckwheat, quinoa), nuts and seeds.

CARBOHYDRATES

Carbohydrates – 'sugars' and fibre – are the body's main fuel providers. The best are complex carbohydrates, found in unrefined foods such as wholemeal bread and pasta, brown rice and fruit and vegetables. Their fibre and nutrient content remains intact, so their energy is released slowly and steadily. This is far preferable to the rapid and fleeting highs provided by refined carbohydrates, such as white bread, white pasta, white rice, and foods high in sugar. Although fibre is not an energy source as such, it benefits the body by supporting the digestive system and helping to eliminate waste and toxins, and keeping energy levels consistent.

THE VEGAN BALANCE OF GOOD HEALTH

(Calories obtained from food)

• Carbohydrate from fruit and vegetables 50%
• Carbohydrate from grains 15%
• Protein 20%
• Total fat 15%
(of which a minimum of essential fats 5%)

The ideal average carbohydrate intake for an adult on a vegan diet is around 65 per cent, with 50 per cent of that coming from fruit and vegetables and 15 per cent from whole grains.

FATS

Fats are rich sources of energy, flavour and fat-soluble vitamins; they help us to feel satisfied after eating, provide insulation to keep us warm, and help protect internal organs. They also play a role in many body processes.

Dietary fats can be divided into two main groups: saturated and unsaturated. Those derived from animals tend to be saturated and usually hard; those derived from plants (except coconut and palm oils) are mainly unsaturated and liquid at room temperature. An excessive amount of saturated fat in the diet can be harmful as it leads to raised cholesterol levels which can be deposited in the arteries and increase the risk of heart disease. Saturated fat can also block the body's conversion of essential fat; as extra saturated fat is not needed by the body it is best avoided.

Unsaturated fats include monounsaturates, for example, olive oil and rapeseed oil, and polyunsaturates, such as sunflower oil and corn oil. Polyunsaturates contain a number of essential fats: particularly important are omega-3 (soya, walnut, rapeseed, hemp and flax) and omega-6 (sunflower and sesame seeds). These fats have a range of functions, including maintenance of the nervous system, the skin and brain function, and the balance of hormones. They are especially important during pregnancy and lactation.

Unsaturated fats are sometimes treated with hydrogen by the food industry to stabilize and harden them, a process that turns them into solid trans fats. These are even more damaging to the body than saturated fats, creating a greater risk of heart disease. Try to avoid them by not eating refined foods.

Saturated fat is sometimes recommended for cooking purposes because it is stable at high temperatures. However, olive oil makes a good substitute, provided it is not heated until it begins to smoke.

Vegan diets are generally beneficially low in saturated fats and high in essential omega 6. However, they can be undesirably low in omega 3 fats unless compensatory steps are taken. Flax or linseed oil is a rich source of omega 3 and can help to give you the desirable 3:1 ratio of omega 6 to omega 3.

Conversion of essential fats within the body also requires other nutrients to be present. These are vitamins B3, B6, biotin and C, and the minerals calcium, magnesium and zinc.

MAIN FOOD GROUPS AT A GLANCE

PROTEIN

Essential for: growth and repair, regulation of most body functions via enzymes, hormones, neurotransmitters and immune cells.

Ideal percentage of diet: 20 per cent
Complete proteins: quinoa, amaranth, buckwheat and soya beans
Complete protein combinations: grains or nuts with legumes; rice or millet with vegetables; vegetables with mushrooms; vegetables with sesame seeds or Brazil nuts

CARBOHYDRATE

Essential for: the body's main fuel providers. Complex carbohydrates also contain fibre which supports the digestive system, helping eliminate wastes and toxins from the body.

Ideal percentage of diet: 65 per cent
50 per cent of daily intake: from fruit and vegetables: beans and peas, brassicas, dark green leafy vegetables, fruits, pumpkin and squashes, root vegetables, seaweeds, sweet peppers
15 per cent of daily intake: from grains: amaranth, brown rice, bulgar wheat, corn, millet, quinoa, rye, wheat, wholegrain breads and pastas

FAT

Essential for: energy. They also carry flavours and fat-soluble vitamins and make us feel full after meals. They also provide insulation, protecting delicate organs. Essential fats are needs for the nervous system, hormones, skin and brain function. They are especially important during pregnancy and beastfeeding for both mother and baby.

Ideal percentage of diet: 15 per cent
Saturated fats: such as palm and coconut oil
Monounsaturated fats: such as olive oil and rapeseed oil
Polyunsaturated fats: omega-3 essential fats including soya beans, walnuts, rapeseed oil, hemp oil, flax oil; omega-6 essential fats including sunflower oil and sesame oil

NUTRIENTS AND THEIR SOURCES

Eat a varied diet and ensure that you incorporate all the nutrients listed below for a chance of living an extra ten healthy years compared with the average omnivore.

VITAMINS

KEY
RDI: Reference Daily Intakes as established by the UK Department of Health 1991 report (1999 reprint) for adults (19–50 years). The first figure is for women, second for men.
SAI: Safe Adequate Intake as established by the UK Department of Health 1991 report (1999 reprint). SAIs are set in the absence of sufficient data for RDIs
SONA: Suggested Optimal Nutritional Amount as set by University of Alabama, USA. Nutrient levels associated with highest health rating.
mg/d : milligrams per day
mcg/d: micrograms per day

VITAMIN A (BETA-CAROTENE)
Essential for: growth, skin, vision, immunity, heart health
Adult RDI: 600–700mcg/d
Adult SONA: 2000mcg/d
Good sources: apricots (dried), carrots, chard, mangoes, melons (yellow), peppers (red and yellow), pumpkin, spinach, squash, strawberries, sweet potatoes, tomatoes, watercress

• VITAMIN B1 (THIAMINE)
Essential for: energy production (from carbohydrates), brain function, digestion
Adult RDI: 0.8-1.0mg/d

Adult SONA: 3.5-9.2mg/d
Good sources: beans and legumes, blackstrap molasses, brown rice, chickpeas, peanuts, soya products, sunflower seeds, wheatgerm, whole grains, yeast extract

• VITAMIN B2 (RIBOFLAVIN)
Essential for: energy production (fats and proteins); skin and internal membranes; nails and hair.
Adult RDI: 1.1–1.3mg/d
Adult SONA: 1.8–2.5mg/d
Good sources: almonds, bamboo shoots, bean sprouts, broccoli, cabbage, green leafy vegetables, mushrooms, pumpkin, soya products, tomatoes, watercress, wheat germ, yeast extract

• VITAMIN B3 (NIACIN)
Essential for: brain and nerve function, skin, energy production, digestion
Adult RDI: 13–17mg/d
Adult SONA: 25–30mg/d
Good sources: asparagus, beets, cabbage, cauliflower, courgettes, fruit (dried), millet, mushrooms, nuts, quinoa, squash, sunflower seeds, tomatoes, wholegrain cereals, yeast extract

• VITAMIN B5 (PANTOTHENIC ACID)
Essential for: energy production, brain and nerve function, skin and hair, helps produce anti-stress hormones
Adult SAI: 3–7mg/d

Adult SONA: 25mg/d
Good sources: alfalfa sprouts, avocados, broccoli, cabbage, celery, corn, lentils, mushrooms, peanuts, peas, tomatoes, soya beans, squash, strawberries, sunflower seeds, tomatoes, sunflower seeds, watercress, whole wheat

• VITAMIN B6 (PYRIDOXINE)
Essential for: protein conversion, growth, nervous and immune systems, heart health (via homocysteine regulation), brain function, hormone production, sex hormone balance
Adult RDI: 1.2–1.4mg/d
Adult SONA: 10–25mg/d
Good sources: avocados, bananas, broccoli, brown rice, Brussels sprouts, cabbage, carrots, cauliflower, red kidney beans, lentils, peppers (green, red and yellow), squash, soya beans, sunflower seeds, walnuts, watercress, wheatgerm, whole grains

• VITAMIN B9 (FOLIC ACID)
Essential for: blood cells, prevention of birth defects, protection against anaemia
Adult RDI: 200 mcg/d
Adult SONA: 400–1000mcg/d
Good sources: asparagus, avocados, Brussels sprouts, bulgur wheat, kidney beans, root vegetables, soya beans, spinach, wheatgerm, whole grains

• VITAMIN B12 (CYANOCOBALAMIN)
Essential for: energy production, nervous

system, prevention of pernicious anaemia, blood-cell formation, heart health (via homocysteine regulation), use of protein
Adult RDI: 1.5mcg/d
Adult SONA: 2–3mcg/d
Good sources: Take a reputable B12 supplement. Small amounts can also be found in breakfast cereals, non-hydrogenated margarines, sausage mixes, fortified soya milks, soya mince, yeast extract

• BIOTIN
Essential for: helping the body use essential fats to aid healthy skin, hair and nerves
Adult SAI: 10–200mcg/d
Adult SONA: 50–200 mg/d
Good sources: almonds, brown rice, cabbage, cauliflower, legumes, lettuce, peas, sweetcorn, tomatoes, whole grains

• VITAMIN C
Essential for: immunity, wound-healing, antioxidant properties, protection against heart disease and cancers, aiding iron absorption
Adult RDI: 40mg/d
Adult SONA: 400–1000mg/d
Good sources: alfalfa sprouts, berries, broccoli, cabbage, citrus fruits, cauliflower, currants, green vegetables, guavas, kale, kiwi fruit, lettuce, mangoes, parsley, peas, peppers (green, red and yellow), pineapple, potatoes, tomatoes

• VITAMIN D
Essential for: healthy bones, protection against osteoporosis
Adult RDI: 10mcg/d
Adult SONA: 10–20mcg/d
Good sources: fortified foods such as breakfast cereals, margarines, soya milk. Sunlight on the skin enables the body to manufacture its own vitamin D. Healthy adult vegans should be able to produce sufficient vitamin D if time is spent outdoors in the spring, summer and autumn

• VITAMIN E
Essential for: antioxidant properties, heart and blood vessel protection, skin immunity, cancer-fighting
Adult SAI: above 3–4mg/d
Adult SONA: 100–1000 mg/d
Good sources: avocado, blackstrap molasses, Brazil nuts, broccoli, cashew nuts, green leafy vegetables, olive oil, peanuts, safflower oil, spinach, sunflower oil, sunflower seeds, sweet potatoes, walnuts, watercress, wheatgerm

• VITAMIN K
Essential for: blood clotting, energy storage, liver function
Adult SAI: 1mcg/kg/d
Adult SONA: 55–80 mcg/d
Good sources: alfalfa, blackstrap molasses, broccoli, cabbage, cauliflower, green leafy vegetables, kelp, lettuce, soya beans, spinach, strawberries, whole grains

MINERALS

• CALCIUM
Essential for: bone formation, prevention of osteoporosis, function of the heart, muscles and nerves
Adult RDI: 700mg/d
Adult SONA: 800–1200mg/d
Good sources: almonds, apples, blackstrap molasses, Brazil nuts, broccoli, chickpeas, seaweed (dried), figs, fortified soya milk, green leafy vegetables, okra, parsley, quinoa, soya beans, swede, tofu, watercress.

• CHROMIUM
Essential for: enabling the body to use glucose and maintain blood sugar levels and for gene expression
Adult SAI: above 25mcg/d
Adult SONA: 100 mcg/d
Good sources: beans, brewer's yeast, nuts, whole grains

• COPPER
Essential for: respiration, nervous system, antioxidant properties, protein metabolism, bone formation
Adult RDI: 1.2mg/d
Adult SONA: not set
Good sources: almonds, avocados, blackstrap molasses, cauliflower, legumes (dried, especially soya beans), green leafy vegetables, nuts, whole grains

• IODINE
Essential for: normal functioning of the thyroid gland, which controls metabolism
Adult RDI: 140mcg/d
Adult SONA: not set
Good sources: green leafy vegetables, iodized salt, pears, seaweed, watercress, wild rice.

• IRON
Essential for: red blood cells, preventing anaemia
Adult RDI: 14.8–8.7mg/d
Adult SONA: 15mg/d
Good sources: apricots (dried), beans, blackstrap molasses, cabbage, dark green leafy vegetables, dates, legumes, millet, nuts, parsley, prunes, pulses, pumpkin seeds, quinoa, raisins, seaweed (dried), sesame seeds, spinach, tofu, wheatgerm, wholemeal bread

• MAGNESIUM
Essential for: energy production, growth and repair, sleep, muscle relaxation
Adult RDI: 270–330mg/d
Adult SONA: 375–500mg/d
Good sources: almonds, bananas, blackstrap molasses, Brazil nuts, broccoli, brown rice, cashew nuts, dark green leafy vegetables, millet, peas, pine nuts, prunes, quinoa, sesame seeds, soya beans, sunflower seeds, wheatgerm, whole grains

• MANGANESE
Essential for: nervous system, sex hormone production, blood sugar regulation, skeletal development

Adult SAI: above 1.4mg/d
Adult SONA: 5mg/d
Good sources: green leafy vegetables, legumes, nuts, pineapple, most seeds, tea, whole grains

• PHOSPHORUS
Essential for: bones, teeth, metabolizing carbohydrates, heart contraction, kidney function
Adult RDI: 550mg/d
Adult SONA: not set
Good sources: broccoli, legumes, nuts, quinoa, whole grains

• POTASSIUM
Essential for: normal cell function, nerves, blood pressure control
Adult RDI: 3500mg/d
Adult SONA: 2000mg/d
Good sources: bananas, blackstrap molasses, chard, fruit (dried, especially apricots), fruit (fresh and juice), millet, nuts, quinoa, raw vegetables, seaweed, soya beans, spinach, sunflower seeds, tomatoes, wholemeal bread, yams

• SELENIUM
Essential for: antioxidant properties, protecting against heart disease and certain cancers, thyroid function
Adult RDI: 60–75mcg/d
Adult SONA: 100mcg/d
Good sources: acorn squash, avocados, Brazil nuts, lentils, mushrooms (fresh or dried), potatoes, sesame and sunflower seeds, walnuts, whole grains
Note: Selenium is dependent on soil levels, so eating organic foods can help

• SODIUM
Essential for: nerve transmission, maintaining body fluid levels
Adult RDI: 1600 mg/d
Adult SONA: 2400 mg/d
Intake: Generally too high. Recommended daily maximum for women is 5g and for men 7g.
Good sources: present in most foods

• ZINC
Essential for: growth, hormone function, male fertility, liver function, immunity, taste, protein digestion
Adult RDI: 7–9.5mg/d
Adult SONA: 15–20mg/d
Good sources: almonds, brown rice, seaweed, lentils, oats, pine nuts, pumpkin, sesame and sunflower seeds, wheatgerm, whole grains, wholemeal bread

NOTES
RDIs are based on minimum levels that prevent deficiency diseases but are not necessarily enough for optimum nutrition. SONAs have also been included to provide this information, where they have been set.

Remember that more is not always better: too much of any nutrient, especially fat-soluble nutrients such as vitamins A, D, E and K can also be damaging.

useful ingredients

The ingredients below are just some of the items that you might find useful to look for when shopping.

Acidophilus The 'live' ingredient in yogurt, acidophilus is the friendly bacteria that ensures your digestive system is working smoothly. It's the arch-enemy of *Candida albicans*, the yeast that can cause upsets if it grows unchecked.

Ackee This tropical fruit comes from an evergreen West African tree and is popular in the West Indies, particularly Jamaica. As the unripe fruit and the parts surrounding it are poisonous, it's probably best to buy it in cans. Similar in flavour and texture to boiled egg yolk, ackee can be used in many dishes, including Thai curries, kedgeree and quiche, or just on toast with a little nutmeg. The Jamaicans add it to a tomato stew.

Agave syrup Sap from the cactus used to make tequila; a good alternative to honey and not usually quite as expensive as maple syrup.

Amaranth and **Quinoa** (pronounced 'keen-wah') Both are pseudo-cereals because the seeds are technically fruits. These Peruvian grains are complete proteins, gluten-free and high in the amino acid lysine. They can be prepared and eaten in the same way as rice, bulgur wheat or couscous.

Avocado oil Deliciously rich and creamy, and excellent for cooking because it has a smoking point higher than most other vegetable oils.

Blackstrap molasses A thick brown residue obtained from sugar cane at the very end of the refining process. Containing iron and vitamin K, it can be used in baking instead of sugar, and combined with hot soya milk to make a delicious bedtime drink.

Bread Best buys are wholegrain and organic.

Calaloo West Indian spinach, often only available in cans. Prepare and use in the same way as spinach or kale.

Cassava Also known as manioc, this thick-skinned root vegetable originally came from Brazil but is now a staple foodstuff in South America and Africa. It may be ground into flour or peeled, chopped and cooked like potatoes. The flavour is similar to that of chestnuts, for which it may be substituted.

Cheese alternatives The characteristic flavours of cheese are sweetness (from lactose), richness (from saturated fat) and salt. Yeast flakes, vegan bouillon powder (Swiss) and vegan vegetable soup mixes with a high yeast content can add a cheesy flavour to sauces and cream made with plant milks. Dark yeast extract can do the same. Many varieties of vegan cheese are now available to buy in supermarkets, but because they are low in sugar, fat and salt many lack taste. There are a few that hit the spot, especially the new vegan cream cheeses, which you can roll in peppercorns, herbs or paprika to make them even more exciting.

Chlorella This comes in supplement or powder form, and is high in phyto (plant) nutrients and B vitamins. It's basically pond-water algae, but you can easily disguise the taste by using the powder in a smoothie.

Chocolate Read the label to ensure the product contains cocoa butter rather than butterfat, and buy the best you can afford.

Cooking oils Use monounsaturates rather than polyunsaturates for cooking. Avocado oil and olive oil are both suitable. You should avoid hydrogenated fats, which contain trans-fatty acids, and keep saturated fats, such as coconut oil and palm oil, to a minimum.

Egg alternatives Among the things that will bind, emulsify or sometimes even taste a bit like eggs are ackee, agar agar, arrowroot, banana, cornflour, rice and powdered plant cellulose, soya flour, tofu and xanthum gum. Rice milk and self-raising flour make lovely pancakes, for instance. You can also buy various manufactured egg substitutes.

Fish alternatives Try smoked tofu, or check out your local healthfood store to find mercury-free, plant-based alternatives to fish. (They are also safe for pregnant women.)

Frozen vegetables Keep a selection in the freezer – they retain their nutrients (unlike fresh vegetables more than a few days old).

Gungo peas A popular pulse in Jamaica, with a taste and texture somewhere between a chickpea and a black-eyed bean. Any bean would do as an alternative.

Hemp seeds The size of grape pips, hemp seeds are very nutritious, with balanced levels of essential omega-3 and 6 oils. They are best eaten raw. Hempseed oil has a nutty flavour and is delicious on salads.

Linseeds Also known as flaxseeds, these tiny seeds are rich in omega 3. Add to cereal, bread and all sorts of dishes.

Meat alternatives Tofu, tempeh and textured vegetable protein are perhaps the most common substitutes for meat, but chestnuts, mushrooms and various combinations of nuts and grains are full of protein and also make good alternatives. Shops now sell a huge variety of meat-free products, from vegan hotdogs to vegan giblet gravy.

Milk alternatives The variety is astonishing, including almond, barley, coconut, oat, pea, quinoa, rice and soya. Try rice milk on cereal, soya milk in sauces, coconut milk in ice cream, oat milk in custard, and any for smoothies.

Mustard A useful ingredient in sauces and dressings. Watch out that your Dijon mustard doesn't contain honey.

Pasta Like bread, buy wholegrain and organic varieties. Apart from the ubiquitous wheat, it is now possible to buy pasta made from almost any grain you can name, including buckwheat, corn and quinoa. Read the label to check eggs aren't among the ingredients.

Pectin The ingredient in certain fruits that helps jam to set. It has good detoxifying properties, and pure fruit pectin can sometimes be used as a gelatine substitute.

Rice Brown basmati rice is the best choice as it is both nutritious and delicious. As with bread, buy wholegrain and organic varieties.

Salad oils Take advantage of all those delicious and nutritious polyunsaturated oils that should be consumed fresh and cold, such as pumpkin, hempseed and walnut.

Seaweed Japanese seaweeds are the best known and can be bought in mixed packs. Arame looks like thick, curly hair, while nori is available as flakes (good for sprinkling on soups or salads, like a herb) or flattened into sheets for making sushi. The Irish, Scots and Welsh maintain that their seaweeds are purer than Japanese varieties. These seaweeds have unique flavours and nutrients, and are a good source of iodine. Try Irish purple dulse (from health food shops or by mail order). Snip it into small pieces and add to stews and rice dishes.

Soya lecithin A natural emulsifier that helps the digestion of essential fats. It also contains choline, which helps to control liver and brain function and cholesterol levels. The granules may be sprinkled into ice cream, smoothies or cereals. Avoid egg lecithin.

Yeast extract A good ingredient for adding a 'meaty' flavour to stews and gravy. Mixed with sweetened soya milk, it can also become quite cheesy in flavour.

Yeast flakes Nutritional yeast has a faintly cheesy flavour and is high in B vitamins. The dried flakes can be added to soups, salads, mash or yogurt, or stirred into a basic white sauce to give it a cheesy flavour. Avoid yeast flakes if you have a digestive disorder arising from candida.

gungo peas

amaranth

calaloo

cassava

ackee

lecithin

chlorella

blackstrap molasses

yeast flakes

basic recipes

vegetable stock

Making your own stock allows you to use seasonal vegetables to vary the flavour.

preparation: 5–10 minutes
cooking: about 35 minutes
makes: 1 litre (1¾ pints)

500 g (1 lb) mixed vegetables, excluding potatoes, parsnips, or other starchy root vegetables, chopped
1 garlic clove
6 peppercorns
1 bouquet garni
1.2 litres (2 pints) water

1 Place all the ingredients in a large saucepan. Bring to the boil and simmer gently for 30 minutes, skimming when necessary.

2 Strain the stock, cool then refrigerate it. It will keep for up to a week in the refrigerator, or up to 3 months in the freezer.

vegan cream cheese

Resembling ricotta, this cheese is especially good on toast with home-made jam. Alternatively, it can be eaten as a savoury – rolled into balls and dipped in herbs, cracked black peppercorns or seaweed flakes.

preparation: 5 minutes
serves: 4

175 g (6 oz) tofu
50 g (2 oz) coconut oil, melted
1 tablespoon rapeseed oil
1 tablespoon lime juice
1 tablespoon agave syrup
2 teaspoons salt

1 Place all the ingredients in a food processor or liquidizer and combine well.

2 Transfer the mixture to a glass jar, store in the refrigerator and use as required. It will keep for up to 1 week.

vegan yogurt

Endlessly versatile, this yogurt can even be frozen.

preparation: 10 minutes, plus cooling and setting
cooking: 5 minutes
serves: 4

500 ml (17 fl oz) sweetened soya milk
2 tablespoons live vegan yogurt (unpasteurized) or 4 vegan acidophilus tablets

1 Sterilize the soya milk by heating it to just below boiling point.

2 Rinse a vacuum flask, large glass jar or sandwich box with boiling water to sterilize it.

3 Once the milk has cooled to lukewarm, pour it into your receptacle, stir in the live yogurt and put the lid on.

4 Place the container near a constant source of low heat, such as in an airing cupboard. Alternatively, wrap it in a towel or newspaper and put it on a hot-water bottle. The yogurt should set within 12 hours. (If the temperature drops too low, it will stop the process or take longer; if the temperature is too high, the bacteria will be killed.)

5 Once set, refrigerate and use within 4–5 days. Keep 2 tablespoons of the yogurt to start off your next batch.

salad dressing

The great thing about this salad dressing, apart from its delicious taste, is that it contains a useful amount of the essential fats necessary for good health.

preparation: 5 minutes
serves: 4

4 tablespoons pumpkin seed oil or hempseed oil
1 tablespoon flax oil
2 teaspoons Dijon mustard
1 tablespoon balsamic vinegar
salt and pepper

1 Mix all the ingredients together and use as required. The dressing will keep for 1 week in the refrigerator.

soyannaise

Of course there's a vegan alternative to mayonnaise – and it tastes just as good as the real thing.

preparation: 5–10 minutes
cooking: 2 minutes
serves: 4

125 ml (4 fl oz) sweetened soya milk
pinch of salt
100 ml (3½ fl oz) sunflower oil
1 dessertspoon white wine vinegar
1 garlic clove, crushed (optional)
1 tablespoon Dijon mustard
25 ml (1 fl oz) flax oil

1 Put the soya milk and salt in a saucepan and heat until hot, but not boiling.

2 While whisking the milk with an electric mixer or hand-held blender, add the oil and vinegar.

3 Still whisking, add the crushed garlic, if using, mustard and flax oil. Refrigerate and use as required. It will keep for up to 1 week.

pizza base

Add any toppings you like to this simple home-made pizza base.

preparation: 10 minutes
cooking: 5 minutes
makes: 1 x 30 cm (12 inch) pizza base

1 tablespoon olive oil, plus extra for oiling
125 g (4 oz) self-raising wholemeal flour
½ teaspoon chopped marjoram
2 dessertspoons rice milk
1 teaspoon wine vinegar
50 ml (2 fl oz) Vegan Yogurt (see page 14)
salt and pepper

1 Oil a baking sheet and preheat the oven to 180°C (350°F), Gas Mark 4. Meanwhile, combine the base ingredients and knead for 10 minutes until smooth and shiny. Roll out to a 30 cm (12 inch) circle, place on the prepared baking sheet and bake for 5 minutes.

2 Remove the pizza base from the oven and brush with oil to make it liquid resistant. Continue with the recipe for the topping.

paprika yogurt dressing

Smoked paprika adds real depth of flavour to this dressing. Try it drizzled over an avocado or mixed-leaf salad

preparation: 5 minutes
serves: 6

250 g (8 oz) soya yogurt
2 tablespoons pumpkin seed oil or hemp oil
1 tablespoon flax oil
1 tablespoon balsamic vinegar
2 tablespoons vegan tomato sauce
1 teaspoon smoked paprika
1 teaspoon finely grated lime rind
salt and pepper

1 Mix all the ingredients together and use immediately.

maple syrup dressing

Being sweet, this dressing is particularly good with the peppery taste of rocket, watercress and baby spinach leaves.

preparation: 4 minutes
serves: 6

2 tablespoons maple syrup
2 tablespoons cider vinegar
2 tablespoons sunflower oil
1 tablespoon soy sauce

1 Mix all the ingredients together and use as required. The dressing will keep for up to 1 week in the refrigerator.

red onion marmalade

Pâtés, vegan cheeses, cold pies, cold nut roast, falafel and hot sausages are all enhanced by a spoonful of this onion marmalade. It is also very good in sandwiches.

preparation: 10–15 minutes
cooking: 50–60 minutes
makes: 1 kg (2 lb)

2 unwaxed oranges, deseeded and finely chopped
250 g (8 oz) chopped red onion
250 ml (8 fl oz) Vegetable Stock (see page 14)
250 g (8 oz) dark brown sugar
4 teaspoons arrowroot
125 ml (4 fl oz) apple pectin

1 Place the oranges, onion and vegetable stock in a medium saucepan, bring to the boil and simmer for 30–40 minutes, until the orange rind is tender.

2 Pour in the sugar and boil furiously for 3–4 minutes, stirring occasionally. Add the arrowroot, stirring continuously as the liquid thickens. Remove the pan from the heat and stir in the pectin.

3 Allow the marmalade to cool a little, then pour into sterilized glass jars. When cold, cover and store until needed.

quick food fixes

Make time to eat and enjoy breakfast, and you will have a head start on the day in terms of nutrition and energy.

Ideally, think about breakfast the night before. Soak some oat flakes in apple juice for porridge, or make sure you have suitable things in the refrigerator or freezer, such as soya milk, sliced wholemeal bread or individual portions of frozen fruit. Try one, or a combination, of the following:

- Cereal bar and fruit juice.
- Mixture of nuts, seeds and fresh or dried fruit.
- Vegan Yogurt (see page 14) with nuts and seeds.
- Warmed wholemeal pitta bread spread with yeast extract or Soyannaise (see page 15) and filled with two vegan sausages or slices of vegan bacon.
- Oatcakes or rice cakes spread with pâté or Vegan Cream Cheese (see page 14) plus fruit.
- Beans on toast.
- Nut butter and yeast extract on toast plus a banana.
- Raw carrot, piece of fruit cake and a glass of fortified plant milk.
- Toasted bagel with mashed tofu and yeast extract.

What do you do for lunch or a snack when you haven't had time to prepare your own? There are lots of vegan options available if you know where to look. Try some of the following:

- Nuts and seeds or Bombay mix.
- Fruit and vegetables, bought ready-prepared, are now available from many different shops.
- Vegan pies, sausages, ice cream and a variety of other treats can be found in most health food shops.
- Samosas, bhajis, pakoras or spring rolls are usually vegan and can be bought from Asian foodshops.
- Hummus (chickpea dip) is delicious with crudités, olives and pitta bread. Roll salad leaves and hummus in a tortilla wrap (minus milk powder).
- Pizza can be bought from a shop or restaurant that allows you to create your own: just leave out the cheese and add lots of nutritious vegetables.

- Salsas with corn tortillas (minus milk powder) make a great lunch.
- Vegan pâté goes well with biscuits, oatcakes or breadsticks, with gherkins, pickle or mustard.
- Vegan sushi, available from upmarket lunch bars.
- Spanish tapas and Greek meze bars offer numerous small dishes that are suitable for vegans.
- Jacket potatoes, topped with anything you like.
- Fresh soups, from sandwich bars or supermarkets, are often OK for vegans. Just check they don't contain any butter or cream.

TOP TEN SANDWICH IDEAS

The sandwich industry is big business, but far too few offerings are suitable for vegans. To redress the balance, here are ten ideas for making lunchtime tastier and more nutritious. Use any kind of bread that takes your fancy, including tortillas and rice pancakes.

- Med Veg: roasted Mediterranean vegetables and olive hummus on sun-dried tomato bread.
- Gentleman's BLT: vegan 'bacon steak' or smoked tofu, lettuce and tomato on thick bread.
- Phillymangerer: Vegan Cream Cheese (see page 14), red peppers, garlic, chopped mangetout and celery.
- Scrambled Meg: Breakfast Scramble (see page 33) with nutmeg and cress.
- Peanut Buttie: peanut butter with yeast extract, vegan coleslaw, bean sprouts and lettuce.
- Sushi Poochi: marinated and baked smoked tofu with sweetcorn, nori seaweed flakes, pickled ginger, lettuce, lemon and capers in rice pancake wraps.
- Fungi Filler: wild mushroom, tarragon and lentil pâté with gherkins, red onion, watercress and alfalfa.
- Falafel-me-gently: chopped falafels, Baba Ghanoush (see page 59), sauerkraut, watercress, spring onion, cucumber and parsley in a wholemeal roll.
- Dolly Pocket: vegan tuna or smoked tofu, capers, nori flakes, vegan tomato pesto, spring onions, salad and Soyannaise (see page 15) in a wholemeal pitta.
- Bloody Mary: cherry tomatoes, sun-dried tomato paste, tahini, red kidney beans, red onion, gherkins. Jalapeño chilli and black pepper in a corn tortilla.

chapter one
breakfasts

preparation: 30–40 minutes, plus chilling and rising
cooking: 10–15 minutes
makes: 6

- 1½ teaspoons fast-action dried yeast
- 1 teaspoon soft brown sugar
- 150 ml (¼ pint) sweetened soya milk, warmed
- 250 g (8 oz) plain flour
- 1 teaspoon salt
- 50 g (2 oz) coconut oil, melted
- 100 g (3½ oz) bar of dairy-free chocolate (optional)
- 1 tablespoon Soyannaise (see page 15), to glaze

croissants

1 Mix the yeast with the sugar and the warm soya milk in a small bowl.

2 Place the flour and salt in a large bowl and mix in half the coconut oil. Make a well in the centre, pour in the yeast mixture and gradually work it in with a fork to make a dough.

3 Flour a work surface and knead the dough for about 10 minutes until smooth. Roll out and spread with the remaining coconut oil. Cut the dough in half, put one half on top of the other, then roll up tightly. Wrap it in a plastic bag and put it in the refrigerator for 30 minutes.

4 When you're ready to make the croissants, divide the chilled dough into 3 pieces and roll each one into a square. Place the squares on separate pieces of baking parchment, roll them up and chill until needed.

5 To make plain croissants, cut the squares in half diagonally, then roll them up loosely from the longest edge towards the point. Bring the 2 ends around to touch each other, making a crescent shape.

6 To make chocolate croissants, place 2 squares of chocolate in the triangles and roll them up as described in step 5.

7 Preheat the oven to 180°C (350°F), Gas Mark 4. Leave the croissants to rise for 30 minutes. Glaze the tops of the croissants with soyannaise and bake for 10–15 minutes, depending how brown you like them.

preparation: 10 minutes
makes: 4 big bars

essential seed snack bars

This recipe is based on Essential Seed Mix, which provides an excellent way of upping your intake of protein and essential fatty acids. It can be used in many different ways – on cereal, in sandwiches, on salads, in soups or even in ice cream – but should not be used in cooking. Here it is used to make delicious snack bars.

Essential seed mix
- 25 g (1 oz) pumpkin seeds
- 25 g (1 oz) sunflower seeds
- 25 g (1 oz) sesame seeds
- 75 g (3 oz) hemp seeds
- 75 g (3 oz) linseeds

Snack bars
- 75 g (3 oz) porridge oats
- 50 g (2 oz) dried dates, finely chopped
- 50 g (2 oz) ready-to-eat dried apricots, finely chopped
- 25 g (1 oz) coconut, finely grated
- 2 teaspoons carob powder
- 1 tablespoon brown rice flour
- 1 tablespoon blackstrap molasses
- 1 tablespoon agave or maple syrup
- 2 tablespoons lime juice

1 To make the essential seed mix, grind the pumpkin, sunflower and sesame seeds in a food processor. Take care not to over-grind, or the sesame will turn to 'putty'. Grind the hemp seeds and linseeds in a herb mill or coffee grinder. Combine the 2 mixtures and transfer to a dark glass jar with a tight-fitting lid. It can be stored in the refrigerator for up to 4 days.

2 Mix all the dry ingredients for the bars in a bowl. Add 4 tablespoons of essential seed mix, the molasses, agave syrup and lime juice and and stir thoroughly.

3 Divide the mixture into 4, then roll into short sausage shapes and pat to flatten into bars.

4 Wrap the snack bars tightly in baking parchment and place in an airtight container. They can be stored in the refrigerator for up to 4 days.

high-protein smoothie

preparation: 5 minutes
serves: 1

Both Canada and the USA claim to have created smoothies back in the 1970s, but the worldwide craze for them didn't really take off until the 1990s. Now smoothie bars are everywhere, but it's easy (and cheaper) to make your own at home.

1 Place all the ingredients in a liquidizer and blend until smooth.

2 Mix in the chlorella algae and yogurt, if using, and serve.

- 1 banana
- ½ mango
- 1 tablespoon Essential Seed Mix (see page 20)
- 1 tablespoon chopped, ready-to-eat mixed dried fruit, e.g. apricots, figs, raisins, peaches, blueberries, banana, papaya, or 2 tablespoons fresh berries
- 250 ml (8 fl oz) soya, rice or oat milk, chilled
- 1 Brazil nut, chopped
- 1 walnut, chopped
- 1 tablespoon chlorella algae (optional)
- 1 tablespoon Vegan Yogurt (optional, see page 14)

high-protein muesli

- 250 g (8 oz) oat flakes
- 100 g (3½ oz) pumpkin seeds
- 100 g (3½ oz) sunflower seeds
- 200 g (7 oz) ready-to-eat mixed dried fruit, e.g. apricots, figs, raisins, blueberries, pineapple, banana, peaches, papaya, chopped
- 6 Brazil nuts, chopped
- 6 walnuts, chopped

It has been claimed that muesli was pioneered in the 1890s by Max Bircher-Benner, a Swiss doctor who called cereals, fruits and vegetables 'food of the sunlight'. As these were then considered food for poor people, his peers gave him quite a hard time. For maximum nutrition, add a dessertspoon of Essential Seed Mix (see page 20) and soya, pea, almond or Quinoa milk to each serving.

1 Mix all the ingredients together and store in an airtight container in a cool, dark place. Serve with slices of fruit or berries and a spoonful of Vegan Yogurt (see page 14).

preparation: 3 minutes
cooking: 15 minutes
serves: 1

- 75 g (3 oz) oats
- 1 tablespoon rapeseed oil
- 1 tablespoon blackstrap molasses
- 1 tablespoon soya milk

toasted granola

This delicious cereal will keep for a few weeks if stored in an airtight container. Serve with soya milk or Vegan Yogurt (see page 14).

1 Preheat the oven to 180°C (350°F), Gas Mark 4. Place all the ingredients in a bowl and stir well so that the oats form clusters.

2 Tip the mixture into a large, shallow tin and bake for 15 minutes.

3 Allow to cool, then store in an airtight container until required.

porridge

preparation: 3 minutes
cooking: 12 minutes
serves: 4

Those on a gluten-free diet can use millet, rice or quinoa instead of oats in this recipe.

1 Place the oats, salt and milk in a large saucepan, bring to the boil, then simmer gently, stirring frequently with a wooden spoon, for about 10 minutes.

2 Stir in the sunflower oil and continue cooking for a further 1–2 minutes.

3 Serve the porridge with small bowls of essential seed mix, chopped dried fruit, maple syrup and soya cream offered separately.

- 125 g (4 oz) porridge oats
- 1 teaspoon salt
- 600 ml (1 pint) rice milk or soya milk
- 1 tablespoon sunflower oil

To serve
- 3 tablespoons Essential Seed Mix (see page 20)
- 4 tablespoons chopped ready-to-eat mixed dried fruit
- 4 tablespoons maple syrup
- 4 tablespoons soya cream

preparation: 5 minutes
cooking: 10 minutes
serves: 4

- **250 g (8 oz) self-raising wholemeal flour**
- **pinch of salt**
- **500 ml (17 fl oz) rice milk or soya milk**
- **1 tablespoon lime juice**
- **rapeseed oil, for frying**

pancakes

This recipe makes fairly thin pancakes; if you prefer very thick ones, use more flour. Stir a handful of raisins into the batter if you like fruity pancakes, which are particularly delicious cold.

1 Mix the flour and salt with the milk and lime juice and beat together to make a smooth batter.

2 Heat a heavy nonstick frying pan until very hot, then pour in a dribble of rapeseed oil and swirl it round the pan.

3 Add just enough pancake mix to barely cover the bottom of the pan in a thin, even layer. Cook for about a minute, until the bottom has set and become lightly browned, then flip the pancake over and cook the other side.

4 Serve the pancakes hot, spread with Vegan Cream Cheese (see page 14) and jam or maple syrup. If you prefer a savoury breakfast, top the pancakes with the cream cheese plus yeast extract and gherkins.

grapefruit salad

- 1 pink grapefruit, halved
  horizontally
- 2 teaspoons soft brown sugar
- ½ teaspoon cinnamon
- 4 tablespoons coconut cream or
  Vegan Yogurt (see page 14)

To serve
- 2 strawberries
- 1 banana, halved
- 1 apple, cored and cut into
  6 segments
- 1 orange, segmented
- 12 seedless grapes
- 1 small papaya, deseeded,
  peeled and cut into segments
- 2 tablespoons berries
- 1 thick slice pineapple, cut
  into 6 segments

Thought to be a mutation of the West Indian pomelo fruit, grapefruit has long been a favourite at breakfast time. The pink-fleshed variety is especially good.

1 Preheat the grill to medium, or preheat the oven to 180°C (350°F), Gas Mark 4. Cut a sliver from the base of each grapefruit half so that they sit level. Cut around the edge of the flesh and between the segments.

2 Mix together the sugar and cinnamon, then rub into the grapefruit flesh. Place the grapefruit halves on a baking sheet and grill for 5 minutes, or heat in the oven for 10 minutes, until the sugar has caramelized.

3 Meanwhile, prepare the strawberries. Starting just below the top to keep the stalk end intact, make several thin cuts right through the berries down to the point. Gently fan out the fruit. Prepare the banana halves in a similar way. Cut wedges from the centre of the apple segments to make 'steps'.

4 Stir any remaining sugar and cinnamon into the coconut cream, then divide between 2 ramekins.

5 Place each grapefruit half on a plate with a ramekin of coconut cream. Arrange the prepared fruit around the edge of the plate, placing a strawberry fan on top of the grapefruit.

creamy mushrooms on toast

preparation: 5 minutes
cooking: 10 minutes
serves: 2

Mushrooms contain B vitamins, calcium, magnesium and zinc, so are a great choice for a healthy breakfast.

1 Preheat the oven to 180°C (350°F), Gas Mark 4. Place the bread on a baking sheet and bake for 5 minutes.

2 Meanwhile, heat the oil in a frying pan, add the lime juice and fry the onion and mushrooms until soft. Stir in the soy sauce, followed by the soya cream.

3 Cut the toast into triangles and arrange on plates in a star shape. Pour the mushroom mix on top, then garnish with a sprinkling of parsley and a slice of lime.

- **4 slices wholemeal bread**
- **1 tablespoon avocado oil**
- **1 tablespoon lime juice**
- **1 small onion, chopped**
- **8 mushrooms, sliced**
- **1 tablespoon soy sauce**
- **2 tablespoons soya cream or Soyannaise or Vegan Yogurt (see page 14 or 15)**

To garnish
- **1 dessertspoon chopped parsley**
- **2 slices of lime**

- 1 dessertspoon soy sauce
- 2 teaspoons avocado oil or olive oil
- 50 g (2 oz) smoked tofu or vegan bacon or ham, finely chopped
- 125 ml (4 fl oz) sweetened soya milk
- 125 ml (4 fl oz) rapeseed oil
- 1 dessertspoon cider vinegar
- 1 tablespoon potato flour
- 1 teaspoon English mustard
- 1 tablespoon vegan tomato sauce
- 1 teaspoon vegan bouillon powder
- 4 slices wholemeal bread
- 1 teaspoon yeast extract
- black pepper

smoky tofu nuggets on toast

1 Preheat the oven to 180°C (350°F), Gas Mark 4. Combine the soy sauce and avocado oil in a small bowl, then add the smoked tofu and mix well. Spoon the tofu mixture on to an oiled baking sheet and place in the oven for 10–15 minutes or until crispy.

2 Heat the soya milk to just below boiling point. Add the rapeseed oil and mix thoroughly with a hand-held whisk. Add the vinegar, whisking all the time.

3 Add the potato flour, mustard, tomato sauce and bouillon powder to the milk mixture, whisk again and bring back to the boil, stirring constantly.

4 Spread the slices of bread with yeast extract.

5 Mix the baked tofu with the milk mixture, then spread on the bread.

6 Place the bread on the baking sheet and bake in the oven for 10 minutes until golden and starting to bubble. Cut each slice into wedges and sprinkle with black pepper.

bubble and squeak

- 2 tablespoons mashed or baked potato
- 2 tablespoons finely chopped red cabbage
- 1 small onion, chopped
- 2 tablespoons self-raising wholemeal flour
- 1 tablespoon olive oil
- 1 tablespoon soya milk
- 1 teaspoon Dijon mustard
- salt and pepper
- 1 tablespoon coconut oil, for frying

Some of the best recipe ideas are based on leftovers and this traditional British recipe is a fine example.

1 Mix all the ingredients together, apart from the oil, and form into 4 burger shapes.

2 Heat the coconut oil in a nonstick frying pan, then fry the burgers on both sides over a medium heat until golden brown.

3 Serve with hot baked beans and mushrooms or scrambled tofu.

breakfast scramble

preparation: 5 minutes
cooking: 15 minutes
serves: 2

Although there are egg replacers available, most of them are binding agents rather than true egg alternatives. The tofu, cauliflower and sweetcorn in this recipe all have whole egg-like properties.

1 Steam the cauliflower for about 10 minutes until soft.

2 Meanwhile, place the sweetcorn and milk in a small saucepan, bring to the boil and simmer for about 5 minutes until soft. Liquidize the mixture or mash with a fork.

3 Add the oil, turmeric, crumbled tofu, cauliflower and salt and pepper, then simmer, stirring, until hot.

4 Toast the bread. Spread the soyannaise on the toast, then top with the steamed cauliflower and tofu mix.

5 To garnish, sprinkle with a pinch of nutmeg and add a sprig of parsley and some tomato wedges.

- 125 g (4 oz) cauliflower, finely chopped
- 3 tablespoons frozen sweetcorn
- 4 tablespoons oat milk
- 1 dessertspoon avocado oil or rapeseed oil
- 1 teaspoon turmeric
- 125 g (4 oz) tofu, crumbled
- 4 slices wholemeal bread
- 1 tablespoon Soyannaise (see page 15)
- salt and pepper

To garnish
- pinch of nutmeg
- sprig of parsley
- tomato wedges

- 4 tablespoons olive oil
- 1 onion, chopped
- 6 mushrooms, sliced
- ½ red pepper, deseeded and chopped
- ½ green pepper, deseeded and chopped
- 50 g (2 oz) tofu, crumbled
- 3 heaped tablespoons strong white flour
- ½ teaspoon baking powder
- 2 heaped teaspoons vegan bouillon powder
- 5 tablespoons soya milk
- 1 tablespoon cider vinegar
- 1 teaspoon mustard
- 1 tablespoon soy sauce
- 2 teaspoons herbes de Provence
- 1 tablespoon Soyannaise (see page 15)
- salt and pepper

egg-free omelette

Although this recipe uses no eggs at all, it's a real winner. For an interesting variation, try adding grated vegan cheese, vegan bacon bits or pumpkin seeds to the mix.

1 Heat 1 tablespoon of the oil in a large nonstick frying pan, then gently fry the onion, mushrooms, peppers and tofu over a medium heat for about 5 minutes, stirring occasionally.

2 Place the flour, baking powder, bouillon powder, milk, vinegar, mustard, soy sauce, herbes de Provence, 2 tablespoons of the oil and salt and pepper in a large jug and whisk with a fork.

3 Fold in the soyannaise, then pour the mixture on to the vegetables in the pan. Cook gently for 3–4 minutes with the pan covered so that the steam partly cooks the top.

4 Slide the omelette on to a plate, then oil the pan, place it upside down over the plate and flip over. Return the pan to the heat and brown the other side of the omelette. Serve hot with a mixed salad.

light meals

preparation: 15 minutes
cooking: about **20** minutes
serves: 2

- 8 teaspoons Vegan Cream Cheese (see page 14)
- 1 garlic clove, chopped
- 1 tablespoon chopped parsley
- 8 peppadew peppers, tops removed and deseeded
- 125 g (4 oz) strong white flour
- 125 ml (4 fl oz) rice milk or soya milk
- 1 tablespoon Vegan Yogurt (see page 14)
- 1 teaspoon arrowroot
- 1 teaspoon vegan bouillon powder
- 1 teaspoon finely grated lime rind
- 1 tablespoon coconut oil
- sesame seeds, for sprinkling

crispy, stuffed peppadew peppers

Peppadew peppers are mild, sweet South African mini peppers. If you can't find them, any baby pepper or large chilli can be used, although you should avoid using scotch bonnet peppers, as they are potently fiery.

1 Oil a baking sheet. Preheat the oven to 180°C (350°F), Gas Mark 4.

2 Place the cream cheese, garlic and parsley in a bowl and mix together thoroughly. Put a teaspoonful of the cream cheese mixture into each of the peppers.

3 Place the flour, milk, yogurt, arrowroot, bouillon powder and lime rind in a small bowl or jug and mix well to make a stiff batter.

4 Dip each stuffed pepper into the batter to coat the outside, then place on the prepared baking sheet.

5 Sprinkle the peppers with the oil and sesame seeds, then bake for about 7 minutes. Baste, then return to the oven for a further 7–10 minutes, until crisp.

preparation: 5 minutes
cooking: 15 minutes
serves: 2

- 1 tablespoon olive oil
- 4 tablespoons frozen sweetcorn
- 2 tablespoons self-raising wholemeal flour
- 1 teaspoon vegan bouillon powder
- 2 tablespoons soya milk
- 1 teaspoon cider vinegar
- 1 dessertspoon chopped chives
- black pepper
- sweet chilli sauce, to serve

corn fritters

For an interesting variation, try adding smoky soya snaps or very finely chopped vegan bacon to the basic sweetcorn mixture.

1 Preheat the oven to 180°C (350°F), Gas Mark 4. Heat 1 teaspoonful of the oil in a frying pan and fry the sweetcorn for a few minutes until it is hot.

2 Combine the flour, bouillon powder, milk, vinegar, chives and pepper in a bowl. Add the sweetcorn to the flour mixture and stir thoroughly.

3 Heat the remaining oil in the frying pan, then add tablespoonfuls of the corn mixture, spacing them well apart. Fry on both sides until light golden brown.

4 Transfer the fritters to a baking tin and bake for 5–10 minutes until they rise a little. Serve with sweet chilli sauce for dipping.

tomato bombs

- **4 large tomatoes**
- **4 tablespoons Vegan Cream Cheese (see page 14)**
- **1 garlic clove, finely chopped**
- **2 tablespoons olive oil**
- **8 plump black olives, pitted and chopped**
- **1 teaspoon finely chopped parsley**
- **1 teaspoon finely chopped marjoram or oregano**
- **salt and pepper**

To garnish
- **Essential Seed Mix (see page 20)**
- **smoked paprika**

These are perfect for a summer lunch. As an alternative, you could stuff the tomatoes with seaweed, sticky rice and smoked tofu for a sushi-type dish.

1 Slice a very thin sliver off the bottom of each tomato so that they sit level on a plate. Cut off the tops and scoop out the seeds and juice into a small bowl. Discard the hard tomato cores.

2 Add the cream cheese, garlic, olive oil, olives, parsley, marjoram and salt and pepper to the bowl of juice and mix well.

3 Stuff the tomatoes with the mixture, taking care not to split them.

4 Garnish the tomatoes with a little essential seed mix and a dusting of smoked paprika. Serve with a mixed salad and ciabatta.

papaya with guacamole

preparation: 15 minutes
cooking: 5 minutes
serves: 4

Papayas are believed to have originated in southern Mexico but are now grown in many parts of the tropics. Their nutritional attributes include useful levels of calcium, magnesium, potassium, vitamin C and beta-carotene.

1 Preheat the oven to 180°C (350°F), Gas Mark 4.

2 Cut the avocado in half, remove the stone and scoop the flesh into a small bowl. Add the yogurt, lime juice, garlic and salt and mix to a smooth consistency using a hand-held mixer or a blender.

3 Wash and dry the papayas, cut them in half, then scoop out the seeds. Cut a sliver off the bottom of each papaya half so that they sit level on individual serving plates.

4 Heat the pitta breads in the oven for about 5 minutes, until warm.

5 Fill each papaya with guacamole and garnish with slices of lime and a sprinkle of smoked paprika. Cut the pitta breads into triangles and arrange around the papaya halves.

- 1 large avocado
- 2 tablespoons Vegan Yogurt (see page 14) or soya milk
- juice of ½ lime
- 1 garlic clove, crushed
- 2 pear-sized papayas
- salt
- 2 wholemeal pitta breads

To garnish
- 1 lime, sliced
- ½ teaspoon smoked paprika

preparation: 5 minutes
cooking: 20–25 minutes
serves: 2

- 2 large flat field mushrooms
- 2 tablespoons olive oil, plus extra for oiling
- 2 spring onions, chopped
- ½ red pepper, deseeded and chopped
- 1 small courgette, chopped
- 4 olives, pitted and chopped
- 2 tablespoons porridge oats
- 1 tablespoon chopped basil
- 1 tablespoon soy sauce
- 1 tablespoon lime juice
- salt and pepper
- mixed salad leaves, to serve

stuffed mushrooms

'Stuffed mushrooms' is not really a strictly accurate name for this dish as the mushrooms are used as a platter or basket for the stuffing. It makes a great dish for a special occasion breakfast or a starter. As a variation, you can use chopped apricots instead of the red peppers and a tart apple instead of the courgette.

1 Preheat the oven to 180°C (350°F), Gas Mark 4. Wipe the mushrooms clean with damp kitchen paper, then remove the stalks and chop them.

2 Heat the oil in a small saucepan and gently fry the chopped mushroom stalks, spring onions, red pepper, courgette, olives and oats until the oats are golden. Stir in the basil, soy sauce and lime juice.

3 Oil the mushroom caps and place them on a baking sheet. Spoon the oat mixture on to the mushrooms, season with salt and pepper, and bake for 15–20 minutes, until the caps start to soften.

4 Serve the hot mushrooms immediately on a bed of mixed salad leaves.

Pancakes
- 75 g (3 oz) self-raising wholemeal flour
- 2 teaspoons Atlantic seaweed flakes or your favourite herbs
- 1 teaspoon smoked paprika
- 350 ml (12 fl oz) rice milk
- ½ teaspoon salt
- black pepper
- avocado oil, for frying
- 2 wedges of lime, to garnish (optional)

Filling
- 8 asparagus spears, trimmed
- 250 ml (8 fl oz) soya milk
- 1 dessertspoon cornflour
- 1 teaspoon vegan bouillon powder
- 1 garlic clove, chopped
- 2 tablespoons vegan port or sherry
- 1 tablespoon olive oil
- 2 teaspoons cider vinegar
- 2 teaspoons Dijon mustard

asparagus pancakes

1 Set the oven to a low heat, about 140°C (275°F), Gas Mark 1. Place all the dry pancake ingredients in a bowl and mix in the rice milk to make a lump-free batter. Cover and chill.

2 Meanwhile, make the filling. Place the asparagus in a vegetable steamer and cook for 10 minutes, until they have softened.

3 Pour the soya milk into a small saucepan, stir in the cornflour and heat until the mixture starts to thicken. Add the remaining ingredients, stirring constantly.

4 To cook the pancakes, heat a frying pan until hot, then pour in a dribble of avocado oil and swirl it around the pan. Whisk the chilled batter, then pour half into the pan, tilting it to spread it out evenly. When the bottom is set and speckled light brown, turn the pancake over and cook the other side. Place in the oven to keep warm, then make the second pancake.

5 To serve, divide the filling between the 2 pancakes, place 4 whole asparagus spears on top of each one, then fold them over and serve immediately on hot plates, garnished with a wedge of lime, if using.

pizza muffins

- 2 muffins or 4 crumpets
- 4 tablespoons vegan tomato sauce
- 4 tablespoons Soyannaise (see page 15)
- 1 teaspoon Dijon mustard
- 1 teaspoon yeast extract
- 1 mushroom, cut into 4 slices
- 4 olives
- salt and pepper

Children love these muffins as party food or just as a snack. Grown-ups might like to replace the muffin with a thick round slice of fried aubergine.

1 Preheat the oven to 180°C (350°F), Gas Mark 4. Split the muffins in half. (If you are using crumpets, leave them whole.)

2 Spread some tomato sauce on each muffin half.

3 Mix together the soyannaise, mustard and yeast extract in a bowl, then place a spoonful on top of each muffin. Put a slice of mushroom and an olive on the top and bake for about 15–20 minutes, until the topping is golden and begins to bubble.

4 Season the muffins with salt and pepper and serve with a mixed green salad or vegan coleslaw.

savoury cookie swirls

preparation: 15 minutes
cooking: 25 minutes
makes: 18

These savoury swirls are very pretty; they make perfect party food and are good for picnics and packed lunches, and children enjoy them too. If you are cooking for people who don't like spicy food, use paprika instead of the chillies.

1 Oil a baking sheet. Preheat the oven to 180°C (350°F), Gas Mark 4.

2 Place the flour, oil, bouillon powder and soya milk in a bowl, mix together to form a dough, then divide into 3 equal pieces. On a floured work surface, roll out the dough into rectangles measuring 15 x 10 cm (6 x 4 inches).

3 Spread the tapenade and chopped mushrooms on one rectangle; the red pesto and chopped red peppers and chillies on another; and the cream cheese, spring onions and herbs on the third.

4 Roll each sheet up from a short end and cut each roll into 6 pieces. Place the savoury swirls on the prepared baking sheet, brush the tops with oil and bake for 25 minutes.

5 Serve the swirls hot with soup or cold with a selection of dips.

- 175 g (6 oz) self-raising wholemeal flour
- 50 ml (2 fl oz) rapeseed oil, plus extra for greasing
- 1 teaspoon vegan bouillon powder
- 125 ml (4 fl oz) soya milk
- 1 tablespoon Seaweed Tapenade (see page 64)
- 2 tablespoons chopped mushrooms
- 1 tablespoon red pesto sauce
- 2 tablespoons chopped red pepper and chillies
- 1 heaped tablespoon Vegan Cream Cheese (see page 14)
- 1 tablespoon chopped spring onions
- 1 tablespoon chopped mixed basil and parsley

preparation: 20 minutes
cooking: 45–50 minutes
serves: 8

- **1 small butternut squash**
- **2 beetroot**
- **1 potato**
- **½ cassava**
- **2 carrots**
- **2 red onions**
- **1 courgette**
- **125 ml (4 fl oz) avocado oil**
- **1 tablespoon soy sauce**
- **4 whole garlic cloves**
- **1 dessertspoon rosemary leaves**
- **1 dessertspoon chopped fennel fronds**
- **salt and pepper**

roasted vegetables

1 Preheat the oven to 180°C (350°F), Gas Mark 4. Scrub and trim all the vegetables, then cut them into finger-sized pieces.

2 Place the avocado oil and soy sauce in a large bowl and mix well. Dip in the vegetable pieces and garlic so that they are well coated.

3 Arrange the squash, beetroot, potato and cassava pieces on a baking tray and bake for 20 minutes.

4 Turn these vegetables over, then add the carrot, onions, courgette and garlic. Sprinkle with the rosemary and fennel, season with salt and pepper, then return the tray to the oven for a further 25–30 minutes.

5 Serve with a variety of dips, such as hummus, Soyannaise (see page 15) or sweet chilli sauce, and some warmed bread.

spicy avocado toast

- 1 tablespoon olive oil
- 4 tablespoons roughly chopped avocado or canned ackee
- 1 onion, finely chopped
- 1 green chilli, finely chopped (optional)
- 2 pinches of nutmeg
- 2 slices rye bread
- 4 teaspoons hempseed oil or pumpkin seed oil
- salt and pepper

To garnish
- 1 dessertspoon chopped parsley or seaweed flakes
- 2 slices of lime

The avocado pear originated in central America and is now an major crop in many parts of the world. A source of vitamin E, it is becoming increasingly important as the source of the perfect healthy cooking oil because of its high level of monosaturated fats.

1 Heat the oil in a small saucepan, then add the avocado, onion, chilli, if using, and nutmeg and season with salt and pepper. Fry gently until the onion is soft.

2 Lightly toast the rye bread.

3 Drizzle the hempseed oil on to the toast, then spoon the hot avocado mixture on top.

4 Arrange the toast on warm plates, sprinkle with parsley and garnish with the lime slices.

pea soufflettes

preparation: **10** minutes
cooking: **25** minutes
serves: **4**

These little soufflés taste great hot or cold, and make a satisfying lunch if served with some mixed leaves and crusty bread. They're also ideal picnic fare.

1 Oil four 8 cm (3¼ inch) ramekins. Preheat the oven to 180°C (350°F), Gas Mark 4.

2 Divide 50 g (2 oz) of the peas between the ramekins and top each one with a teaspoon of yogurt.

3 Place all the remaining ingredients, apart from the vinegar, in a bowl, and mix thoroughly using a hand-held mixer or a blender. Add the vinegar and mix again.

4 Pour the mixture into the ramekins and bake for about 25 minutes, until golden brown on top and a cocktail stick inserted in the middle comes out clean.

- 200 g (7 oz) frozen peas
- 4 teaspoons Vegan Yogurt (see page 14)
- 150 g (5 oz) self-raising wholemeal flour
- 1 tablespoon rapeseed oil
- 2 teaspoons vegan bouillon powder
- 1 tablespoon chopped apple mint
- 200 ml (7 fl oz) sweetened soya milk
- 1 tablespoon cider vinegar

crispy duckless pancakes

preparation: 10 minutes
cooking: 20–25 minutes
serves: 4

- 1 tablespoon soy sauce
- 1 tablespoon blackstrap molasses
- 2 tablespoons avocado oil
- 250 g (8 oz) mock duck or tofu, crumbled
- 1 onion, finely chopped
- 6 mushrooms, sliced
- 12 rice pancakes, fresh or dried
- 2 tablespoons sesame seeds
- 1 cucumber, sliced into short lengths
- 6 spring onions, sliced into lengths
- 1 lime, quartered
- 6 tablespoons vegan oyster sauce

Mock duck is a meat substitute from the Far East. It is readily available in cans and may also be found frozen, in a duck shape, in Chinese supermarkets. If using dried rather than fresh rice pancakes, provide individual bowls of hot water so that people can soak their own pancakes for 30 seconds as they need them. Afterwards the water can be used for rinsing sticky fingers.

1 Oil a baking sheet. Preheat the oven to 180°C (350°F), Gas Mark 4.

2 Mix the soy sauce, molasses and oil in a bowl, then add the mock duck, onion and mushrooms and stir thoroughly to coat.

3 Place a thin layer of the mock duck mixture on the prepared baking sheet and bake for 20–25 minutes, until crispy.

4 Heat the rice pancakes according to the packet instructions.

5 Place the mock duck, sesame seeds, cucumber, spring onions, lime and oyster sauce in separate serving bowls.

6 At the table, spread a teaspoonful of oyster sauce on a warm pancake. Top with a spoonful of mock duck, a few sticks of cucumber, a spoonful of spring onion, a sprinkling of sesame seeds and a squeeze of lime juice, then roll up and eat.

potato, sea vegetable and leek soup

preparation: 10 minutes
cooking: 20 minutes
serves: 4

- 2 potatoes, scrubbed and chopped
- 500 ml (17 fl oz) Vegetable Stock (see page 14)
- 2 leeks, finely chopped
- 250 ml (8 fl oz) rice milk
- 2 garlic cloves, chopped
- 2 tablespoons olive oil
- 2 tablespoons mixed Atlantic sea vegetable flakes or finely chopped dulse
- 2 teaspoons mustard powder
- 2 tablespoons cider vinegar
- 1 dessertspoon miso paste
- salt and pepper

To garnish
- pumpkin seed oil
- Essential Seed Mix (see page 20)

The addition of sea vegetables to the old favourite, potato and leek soup, not only adds extra flavour and texture, it also enhances the nutritional value of the dish. As they contain calcium, iron and potassium, sea vegetables are good for heart health and can help rid the body of toxins.

1 Place the potatoes and vegetable stock in a large saucepan, bring to the boil and simmer for 10 minutes.

2 Add all the remaining ingredients and simmer for a further 10 minutes. Transfer to a food processor or liquidizer and blend to a smooth consistency.

3 Serve the soup in warm bowls with a drizzle of pumpkin seed oil and a sprinkling of essential seed mix, and accompanied by warm ciabatta.

broccoli and peanut soup

preparation: 10 minutes
cooking: 15–20 minutes
serves: 4

Broccoli really is a wonder food and has enjoyed great success in many studies investigating protection against a range of diseases including heart disease and Alzeimer's. It has revered antioxidant properties and contains calcium, magnesium, phosphorus, vitamins B3, B5, C and beta-carotene and high levels of folic acid.

1 Place the broccoli, onion and oat milk in a large saucepan, bring to the boil and simmer for 10–15 minutes, until softened.

2 Transfer the mixture to a food processor or liquidizer and blend to a smooth consistency. Add the oil, bouillon powder and peanut butter and season with salt and pepper, then blend again. With the processor or liquidizer still running, add the cider vinegar.

3 Return the soup to the pan and reheat gently. Serve in warm bowls with hot, crusty bread and a sprinkling of essential seed mix.

- 300 g (10 oz) purple-sprouting broccoli, chopped
- 1 onion, chopped
- 600 ml (1 pint) oat milk or soya milk
- 2 tablespoons olive oil
- 1 tablespoon vegan bouillon powder
- 2 tablespoons peanut butter
- 2 tablespoons cider vinegar
- salt and pepper
- Essential Seed Mix (see page 20), to garnish

- 6 medium beetroot, peeled and chopped
- 1 tablespoon lime juice
- 125 g (4 oz) ready-to-eat dried apricots, chopped
- 2 red onions, chopped
- 1 garlic clove, chopped
- 1 teaspoon cumin
- 1 teaspoon paprika
- 1.2 litres (2 pints) Vegetable Stock (see page 14)
- 600 ml (1 pint) orange juice
- salt and pepper

To garnish
- soya cream
- 2 tablespoons pumpkin seed oil
- 2 tablespoons chopped coriander leaves

apricot, beetroot and cumin soup

The purée base of this soup is ideal for freezing in individual portions. For a quick and tasty lunch, simply defrost, dilute with orange juice and heat through.

1 Place the beetroot, lime juice, apricots, onions, garlic, cumin, paprika and vegetable stock in a large saucepan. Bring to the boil, then cover and simmer gently for 45 minutes.

2 Transfer the mixture to a food processor or liquidizer and blend until smooth. (The soup can be frozen at this point.)

3 Add the orange juice, then season to taste with salt and pepper. Garnish the soup with a swirl of soya cream, a little pumpkin seed oil and a sprinkling of coriander leaves.

tomato and orange soup with garlic ciabatta

preparation: 10 minutes
cooking: 20–25 minutes
serves: 4

- 2 tablespoons avocado oil
- 2 garlic cloves, chopped
- 4 ready-to-bake ciabatta rolls
- 2 tablespoons olive oil
- 1 red onion, chopped
- 2 carrots, chopped
- 1 kg (2 lb) tomatoes, chopped
- 1 red pepper, deseeded and chopped
- 1 small red chilli pepper, deseeded and chopped
- 1 tablespoon paprika
- 1 tablespoon cider vinegar
- 4 ready-to-eat dried apricots, chopped
- 500 ml (17 fl oz) orange juice
- 50 ml (2 fl oz) ginger wine
- salt and pepper

To garnish
- soya cream
- 1 tablespoon chopped parsley

1 Preheat the oven to 180°C (350°F), Gas Mark 4. Place the avocado oil, garlic and salt and pepper in a small jug and mix well.

2 Slice the rolls in half and spread with the garlic oil. Wrap in foil and bake for 15 minutes.

3 Meanwhile, heat the olive oil in a large saucepan and gently fry the onion and carrots until the onions are soft. Add the tomatoes, red pepper and chilli. Heat for a few minutes to soften.

4 Stir in the remaining ingredients, then transfer to a food processor or liquidizer and blend until smooth.

5 Return the soup to the saucepan and heat gently for 5–10 minutes, until hot. Garnish with a drizzle of soya cream and a sprinkling of chopped parsley and serve with the hot garlic ciabatta.

baba ghanoush

preparation: **10** minutes
cooking: **30** minutes
serves: **4**

This creamy aubergine dip is a favourite throughout the Middle East. The aubergines are sometimes chargrilled but this is not essential.

1 Preheat the oven to 200°C (400°F), Gas Mark 6. Halve the aubergines lengthways, brush the cut side with olive oil and bake for about 30 minutes, until soft.

2 Scoop out the flesh of the aubergines, transfer it to a food processor or liquidizer, then add the remaining ingredients and blend until smooth. Transfer the mixture to a serving bowl, cover and chill until required.

3 Just before serving, dust the purée with smoked paprika and garnish with olives and slices of lime. Serve with warm pitta bread or oatcakes, and a selection of crudités for dipping.

- 2 aubergines
- 2 tablespoons olive oil
- 1 dessertspoon tahini
- 1 tablespoon balsamic vinegar
- 1 garlic clove, chopped
- 1 teaspoon ground cumin
- juice of ½ lime
- 1 tablespoon Vegan Yogurt or Soyannaise (see pages 14 and 15)

To garnish
- smoked paprika
- olives
- slices of lime

courgettes stuffed with lentil and walnut pâté

preparation: 15 minutes
cooking: 45–50 minutes
serves: 4

- 4 courgettes
- 1 tablespoon avocado or olive oil
- 1 tablespoon soy sauce

Pâté
- 125 g (4 oz) red lentils
- ½ onion, chopped
- 1 garlic clove, chopped
- 250 ml (8 fl oz) Vegetable Stock (see page 14)
- 25 g (1 oz) shelled walnuts, chopped
- 1 teaspoon cider vinegar
- 1 teaspoon yeast extract
- 1 dessertspoon chopped dates
- 1 tablespoon rapeseed oil
- 1 teaspoon soya milk
- 1 teaspoon chopped thyme

1 Preheat the oven to 180°C (350°F), Gas Mark 4. First make the pâté. Fill a medium saucepan with cold water, add the lentils and bring to the boil.

2 Drain the lentils, rinse under running cold water, then return them to the saucepan. Add the onion, garlic and vegetable stock, bring to the boil, then simmer for 20 minutes.

3 Drain the lentils again, then stir in all the remaining pâté ingredients, transfer the mixture to a food processor or liquidizer and blend until smooth.

4 Slice a thin sliver from the bottom of the courgettes so that they sit level on a plate. Cut a rectangle almost the length and width of the courgettes through the skin on the top side. Carefully remove the rectangle of skin, then scoop out the flesh using a teaspoon. (Freeze the flesh for use in another recipe at a later date.)

5 Mix together the oil and soy sauce, then brush the cut surfaces of the courgettes with it. Bake for about 15 minutes. Remove the courgettes from the oven, fill with the lentil pâté and return to the oven for 5–10 minutes to heat through.

6 Serve with a mixed salad, Red Onion Marmalade (see page 16) and warm oatcakes.

butter bean and pumpkin seed dip

preparation: 8 minutes
serves: 4–6

- 250 g (8 oz) cooked butter beans
- 50 g (2 oz) pumpkin seeds
- 2 tablespoons lime juice
- pinch of sea salt
- 1 tablespoon flax oil
- 1 tablespoon olive oil
- 1 garlic clove, chopped
- 2 tablespoons Vegan Yogurt (see page 14) or soya milk

To garnish
- 1 tablespoon chopped parsley
- 1 teaspoon cumin seeds

Healthy food rarely tasted this good in the early days of vegetarianism! In this dip, we have zinc, calcium, iron, magnesium, various B vitamins, phosphorus, potassium, omega 3 and other essential fatty acids.

1 Place all the ingredients in a food processor or liquidizer and blend to a smooth consistency.

2 Transfer the dip to a serving bowl and garnish with the parsley and cumin seeds.

3 Serve with Roasted Vegetables (see page 48) or crudités, and warm pitta bread or oatcakes.

smoked tofu and horseradish pâté

preparation: 7 minutes
serves: 2–4

Tofu is very versatile and when it's smoked or marinated it takes on a life of its own. Here, with the addition of horseradish, the smoked tofu becomes almost fishy without tasting fishy.

1 Place all the ingredients in a food processor or liquidizer and blend to a smooth consistency.

2 Transfer the pâté to a serving bowl and garnish with smoked paprika and slices of lime.

3 Serve with Roasted Vegetables (see page 48) or crudités, and warm pitta bread or oatcakes.

- 125 g (4 oz) smoked tofu
- 2 teaspoons tamarind paste
- 1 teaspoon smoked paprika
- 1 tablespoon lime juice
- 1 tablespoon flax oil
- 1 teaspoon grated horseradish
- 2 teaspoons capers
- 2 teaspoons seaweed flakes
- salt and pepper

To garnish
- smoked paprika
- slices of lime

- 25 g (1 oz) arame or mixed
  Atlantic seaweeds
- 2 tablespoons lime juice
- 1 teaspoon tamarind paste
- 1 teaspoon miso paste
- 1 tablespoon blackstrap
  molasses
- 1 tablespoon flax oil
- 1 tablespoon olive oil
- 1 tablespoon capers
- 1 garlic clove, chopped
- 1 tablespoon pitted and
  chopped large black olives
- 1 tablespoon soya milk
- 1 heaped teaspoon tahini
- 1 teaspoon carob powder
- black pepper
- Vegan Cream Cheese (see page
  14), to serve (optional)

seaweed tapenade

The Provençal condiment on which this recipe is based contains anchovies. The seaweed used in this version has a similarly strong flavour, so use only a little at a time. It does not need salt because several of the ingredients are very salty. This tapenade makes great party food: use it to stuff cherry tomatoes or celery sticks, or mix with equal quantities of Vegan Cream Cheese (see page 14) for canapés or as a quick snack (as illustrated).

1 Place the seaweed in a dish with the lime juice and leave to soak for about 30 minutes, until soft.

2 Place all the remaining ingredients in a food processor or liquidizer and blend to a smooth consistency.

3 Transfer the tapenade to a serving bowl, mix with cream cheese, if using, and serve with oatcakes and cherry tomatoes.

millet salad

- 125 g (4 oz) millet seeds
- 300 ml (½ pint) Vegetable Stock (see page 14)
- 2 teaspoons balsamic vinegar
- 1 teaspoon olive oil
- 2 tablespoons lime juice
- pinch of salt
- 2 spring onions, chopped
- 50 g (2 oz) green beans, chopped
- 2 dessertspoons chopped dried fruit
- 2 dessertspoons pumpkin seeds
- 2 dessertspoons sunflower seeds
- 50 g (2 oz) ready-to-eat dried apricots, chopped
- 1 bunch of watercress, chopped
- chopped herbs, to garnish

Despite mocking associations with bird food, millet is a good, low-allergenic, gluten-free grain; it is highly alkaline and easily digestible.

1 Place the millet seeds and vegetable stock in a small saucepan, bring to the boil and simmer for 25 minutes.

2 Rinse the millet under cold running water and drain in a sieve.

3 Transfer the millet seeds to a bowl, add the remaining ingredients, then cover and chill until required.

4 Garnish the millet with fresh herbs and serve with warm pitta bread or in a tortilla wrap.

sea-fruit cocktail

preparation: **10** minutes
cooking: **25** minutes
serves: **4**

Vegan prawns are available from Chinese, Thai and Korean food shops. They require no preparation before cooking. If not available, use 125 g (4 oz) dried soya chunks or 250 g (8 oz) smoked tofu.

1 If using dried soya chunks, boil them in water for 20 minutes with 2 tablespoons cider vinegar and 1 teaspoon salt, then allow to cool. If using smoked tofu, toss the pieces in 1 tablespoon each of soy sauce and avocado oil, and bake in a preheated oven, 180°C (350°F), Gas Mark 4, for 25 minutes. Allow to cool.

2 Place the vegan prawns, soya chunks or smoked tofu in a large serving bowl, add all the remaining salad ingredients and mix well.

3 Spoon the salad mixture on to lettuce leaves and garnish with the lime, tomatoes, avocado and a sprinkling of nori flakes. Serve with warm granary bread.

- 250 g (8 oz) packet vegan prawns
- 8 tablespoons Paprika Yogurt Dressing (see page 16)
- 2 tablespoons capers
- 2 dessertspoons mixed Atlantic seaweed flakes or flaked nori
- 8 lychees, peeled, stoned and quartered
- 1 spring onion, chopped
- 1 large sweet pickled cucumber, finely chopped
- pinch of sea salt
- 1 garlic clove, finely chopped
- ½ teaspoon smoked paprika
- 2 teaspoons chopped parsley

To garnish
- 1 lime, quartered
- 8 cherry tomatoes
- 2 avocados, halved, stoned, peeled and cut into fans
- nori flakes

chapter three
main meals

preparation: 20 minutes
cooking: 35 minutes
serves: 4

artichoke pizza

Pizza base (see page 15)

Tomato topping
• 400 g (13 oz) can tomatoes
• 1 onion, chopped
• 2 garlic cloves, chopped
• 1 teaspoon chopped oregano
• 1 bay leaf
• 1 red and 1 green pepper, deseeded and chopped
• 1 carrot, grated
• ¼ cabbage, finely sliced
• 1 tablespoon olive oil
• 1 tablespoon balsamic vinegar
• 6 mushrooms, sliced

To garnish
• 6 canned artichoke hearts
• black olives
• 6 strips baked smoked tofu

'Cheesy' topping
• 125 ml (4 fl oz) soya milk
• 50 ml (2 fl oz) avocado oil
• 1 tablespoon cider vinegar
• 50 g (2 oz) coconut oil
• 1 dessertspoon vegan bouillon powder
• 1 boiled potato
• 1 teaspoon Dijon mustard
• 1 teaspoon chilli sauce
• 1 tablespoon tomato sauce

1 Prepare and cook the pizza base following the instructions on page 15.

2 Place the tomatoes in a food processor and blend until smooth. Transfer to a large saucepan, add the onion, garlic, oregano and bay leaf. Bring to the boil, then simmer gently for about 20 minutes.

3 Stir the remaining tomato topping ingredients into the pan, then transfer the mixture to the oiled pizza base, bringing it right up to the edges. Arrange the garnish ingredients on top, then return the pizza to the oven for 5 minutes.

4 To make the 'cheesy' topping, heat the soya milk until hot but not boiling, then pour it into a food processor or liquidizer. Add the oil and vinegar and blend well. Add the remaining 'cheesy' topping ingredients, then spread the mixture over the pizza.

5 Raise the oven temperature to 200°C (400°F), Gas Mark 6 and bake the pizza for another 5–10 minutes, until the topping starts to bubble and turn golden brown. Serve with a crisp dressed salad.

seaweed quinoa kedgeree

- **250 g (8 oz) quinoa seeds**
- **500 ml (17 fl oz) Vegetable Stock (see page 14)**
- **15 g (½ oz) dried arame seaweed**
- **3 tablespoons olive oil**
- **1 onion, chopped**
- **250 g (8 oz) smoked tofu, chopped**
- **250 g (8 oz) avocado, roughly chopped**
- **2 garlic cloves, chopped**
- **½ teaspoon cayenne pepper**
- **2 tablespoons soy sauce**
- **100 g (3½ oz) green beans, chopped**
- **1 tablespoon capers**
- **1 red pepper, deseeded and chopped**
- **juice of 1 lime**
- **1 tablespoon chopped coriander leaves**
- **salt and pepper**

To garnish
- **4 sprigs of parsley**
- **1 lime, cut into wedges**
- **nori flakes**
- **chilli sauce (optional)**
- **smoked paprika**

1 Place the quinoa and vegetable stock in a saucepan and bring to the boil. Reduce the heat, add the arame and simmer gently for 20 minutes, until the quinoa has absorbed the liquid and is light and fluffy.

2 Meanwhile, heat the oil in a frying pan and gently fry the onion and smoked tofu until the tofu begins to brown.

3 Add the avocado, garlic, cayenne pepper, soy sauce and salt and pepper and cook, stirring, until hot.

4 Add the beans, capers, red pepper and lime juice. Stir well, then add the mixture to the pan of quinoa. Fold in the coriander.

5 Transfer the kedgeree to a serving bowl and garnish with sprigs of parsley, wedges of lime, nori flakes, chilli sauce, if using, and a sprinkling of smoked paprika. Serve with a crisp green salad.

ackee quiche

preparation: 15 minutes
cooking: 25 minutes
serves: 4

1   Oil a 20 cm (8 inch) pie dish. Preheat the oven to 200°C (400°F), Gas Mark 6.

2   First make the pastry. Place the flour in a bowl, add the oil and salt and mix with a fork. Add the milk and mix to make a firm dough.

3   Flour a work surface and briefly knead the dough. Roll it out and use to line the prepared dish. Bake for 5 minutes.

4   To make the filling, heat 2 tablespoons of the oil in a frying pan and fry the mushrooms, onion and ackees.

5   Place the yogurt, bouillon powder, tomato purée, mustard and the remaining olive oil in a small bowl and mix well.

6   Put the ackee mixture into the pie shell, spoon the yogurt mixture over the top, then garnish with the sliced tomato. Bake for 20 minutes, or until the top begins to bubble and brown.

7   Garnish the finished quiche with sprigs of parsley and a sprinkling of smoked paprika. Serve with a crisp green salad and some roasted sweet potatoes.

Pastry
- **250 g (8 oz) self-raising wholemeal flour**
- **60 ml (2½ fl oz) rapeseed oil**
- **pinch of salt**
- **60 ml (2½ fl oz) soya milk**

Filling
- **3 tablespoons olive oil**
- **100 g (3½ oz) mushrooms, chopped**
- **1 onion, chopped**
- **250 g (8 oz) canned ackees, drained**
- **125 ml (4 fl oz) Vegan Yogurt or Soyannaise (see pages 14 or 15)**
- **2 teaspoons vegan bouillon powder**
- **1 teaspoon tomato purée**
- **1 tablespoon Dijon mustard**
- **1 large tomato, sliced**

To garnish
- **sprigs of parsley**
- **smoked paprika**

Pastry

- 300 g (10 oz) self-raising wholemeal flour
- 1 teaspoon vegan bouillon powder
- 125 ml (4 fl oz) rapeseed oil
- 125 ml (4 fl oz) rice milk or soya milk

Filling

- olive oil, for oiling and frying
- 1 medium cauliflower, broken into florets
- 125 g (4 oz) asparagus, trimmed and washed
- 2 red onions, chopped
- 50 g (2 oz) shiitake mushrooms, sliced
- 125 g (4 oz) frozen sweetcorn, mashed
- 250 ml (8 fl oz) sweetened soya milk
- 250 ml (8 fl oz) rapeseed oil
- juice of 1 lime
- 2 tablespoons porridge oats
- 2 dessertspoons vegan bouillon powder
- 2 tablespoons vegan tomato sauce
- 1 tablespoon Dijon mustard
- smoked paprika
- black pepper

cauliflower and asparagus tart

1 Oil a 30 cm (12 inch) flan or pie dish. Preheat the oven to 180°C (350°F), Gas Mark 4.

2 To make the pastry, place the flour and bouillon powder in a bowl and rub in the oil, then mix in the milk. Knead the pastry gently for a few moments, then roll out on a floured surface and use it to line the prepared dish. Bake for 10–15 minutes, until just cooked through.

3 Meanwhile, steam the cauliflower and asparagus until hot but not cooked – about 4–5 minutes.

4 Heat a little olive oil in a frying pan and fry the onions and mushrooms until soft. Add the mashed sweetcorn and stir until hot.

5 Heat the soya milk in a saucepan until hot but not boiling. Transfer to a food processor or liquidizer, add the rapeseed oil, season with pepper and mix well. With the machine still running, add the lime juice and mix thoroughly to prevent curdling.

6 Add the oats, bouillon powder, tomato sauce and mustard to the milk mixture and blend again.

7 Oil the inner base of the pie crust, then spread a thin layer of the oat mixture over it. Place a layer of the mushroom mixture on top, then a layer of the cauliflower, followed by the remaining oat mixture.

8 Arrange the asparagus spears on top and sprinkle with smoked paprika. Return the tart to the oven and cook for a further 20 minutes. Serve with a green salad.

caribbean crumble

It's thought that the Spanish conquistadors were responsible for introducing Jamaica to gungo peas. The variety of chilli suggested is very hot, so omit it if you dislike spicy food.

Filling
- 400 g (13 oz) can tomatoes
- 2 onions, chopped
- 1 sweet potato, chopped
- 1 red and 1 green pepper, deseeded and chopped
- 200 g (7 oz) vegan prawns or smoked tofu, cubed
- 250 g (8 oz) gungo peas, cooked
- 1 teaspoon finely chopped fresh root ginger
- ¼ teaspoon ground nutmeg
- 1 Scotch bonnet chilli pepper, deseeded and finely chopped (optional)
- salt and pepper

Crumble
- 125 g (4 oz) wholemeal flour
- 75 g (3 oz) porridge oats
- 2 tablespoons desiccated or freshly grated coconut
- 25 ml (1 fl oz) rapeseed oil
- 25 ml (1 fl oz) soya milk
- salt and pepper

To garnish
- ½ small pineapple, cored, peeled and chopped
- ½ small mango, stoned, peeled and chopped
- desiccated or freshly grated coconut, for coating

1   Preheat the oven to 180°C (350°F), Gas Mark 4. Place the tomatoes in food processor or liquidizer and blend until smooth. Transfer them to a medium saucepan, add the onions and bring to the boil, then lower the heat and simmer for 5 minutes. Add all the remaining filling ingredients to the pan and stir thoroughly.

2   Place all the dry crumble ingredients in a food processor or bowl. Add the oil and milk, season with salt and pepper and process or rub together until the mixture resembles crumbs.

3   Divide the tomato mixture between six ovenproof dishes and top evenly with the crumble. Bake for 30 minutes.

4   To serve, garnish the crumble with pieces of pineapple and mango dipped in grated coconut.

millet pasties

preparation: 20 minutes
cooking: 50 minutes
serves: 4

1 Oil a baking sheet and preheat the oven to 180°C (350°F), Gas Mark 4. Place the flour and bouillon powder in a bowl, add the oil and soya milk and mix together with a fork. Knead gently for a few moments, then cover and chill until needed.

2 Pour the millet and vegetable stock into a saucepan, bring to the boil, then simmer for 20 minutes.

3 Meanwhile, place the potato and carrot in another saucepan, add just enough water to cover, then bring to the boil and simmer for 10 minutes. Add the green beans and cauliflower and simmer for another 5 minutes. Strain the vegetables, then add to the millet along with the onion, sage, yeast extract, black pepper, bouillon powder, lime juice and mustard.

4 Take the chilled pastry and divide into 4 equal pieces. Flour a work surface and roll each piece into a circle about 15 cm (6 inches) in diameter.

5 Place a tablespoon of the millet mixture on each circle, then bring the edges of the pastry together to make a half-moon shape, and press firmly with your fingers to seal.

6 Place the pasties on the prepared baking sheet, brush them with the soyannaise and bake for 30 minutes. Serve hot with Roasted Vegetables (see page 48) or cold with a green salad.

Pastry
- **250 g (8 oz) plain flour**
- **½ teaspoon vegan bouillon powder**
- **75 ml (3 fl oz) rapeseed oil**
- **125 ml (4 fl oz) soya milk**
- **1 tablespoon Soyannaise (see page 15), to glaze**

Filling
- **50 g (2 oz) millet seeds**
- **150 ml (¼ pint) Vegetable Stock (see page 14)**
- **1 potato, chopped**
- **1 carrot, chopped**
- **50 g (2 oz) green beans, chopped**
- **50 g (2 oz) cauliflower, chopped**
- **½ onion, chopped**
- **1 teaspoon sage**
- **1 teaspoon yeast extract**
- **½ teaspoon black pepper**
- **1 teaspoon vegan bouillon powder**
- **juice of ½ lime**
- **1 tablespoon mild mustard**

preparation: 10 minutes
cooking: 30–35 minutes
serves: 4

inca parcels

- 200 g (7 oz) amaranth
- 500 ml (17 fl oz) Vegetable Stock (see page 14)
- 8 cabbage or vine leaves
- 20 large black olives, pitted and quartered
- 1 garlic clove, crushed
- 2 pickled jalapeño peppers, chopped
- 1 tablespoon seaweed flakes
- 1 tablespoon pumpkin seed oil
- 1 dessertspoon balsamic vinegar
- 1 teaspoon smoked paprika
- salt and pepper
- 8 cocktail sticks
- avocado oil, for brushing

1 Preheat the oven to 180°C (350°F), Gas Mark 4. Place the amaranth and vegetable stock in a medium saucepan and bring to the boil. Simmer for about 25 minutes, until the amaranth is tender and all the stock has been absorbed.

2 Meanwhile, steam the cabbage leaves for a few minutes until limp.

3 Add the olives, garlic, jalapeño peppers, seaweed flakes, pumpkin seed oil, vinegar, paprika and salt and pepper to the amaranth pan.

4 Place a dessertspoonful of the mixture on each cabbage leaf, fold it into a parcel and spear with a cocktail stick.

5 Brush each parcel with avocado oil and bake for 5–10 minutes, until hot. Serve with a tomato, red onion and tofu salad and mixed leaves.

pasta-leeky

- 250 g (8 oz) gluten-free pasta
- 125 g (4 oz) tofu
- 2 leeks, chopped
- 3 garlic cloves, chopped
- 125 g (4 oz) frozen peas
- 8 mushrooms, sliced
- 50 g (2 oz) shelled walnuts, chopped
- 1 bay leaf
- 1 teaspoon chopped thyme
- 500 ml (17 fl oz) soya or oat milk
- 1 dessertspoon cornflour
- juice of 1 lime
- 2 teaspoons chopped coriander leaves
- black pepper

A gluten-free pasta dish so deliciously creamy and nutty that everyone will want some. Free of oil, sugar and salt too, it's also ideal for those on a detox diet.

1 Place the pasta in a pan of cold water, bring to the boil, stir, then set aside (off the heat) with a lid on.

2 Place the tofu, leeks, garlic, peas, mushrooms, walnuts, bay leaf, thyme and milk in a large pan, bring to the boil and simmer for about 10 minutes.

3 Put the cornflour in a small bowl, add the lime juice and stir until smooth.

4 Take the vegetables off the heat and stir in the cornflour mixture until the sauce thickens.

5 Drain the pasta, add it to the vegetables and reheat.

6 Stir in the coriander and black pepper, then serve in deep dishes garnished with red onion rings or apple slivers. Those not on a detox diet might like to drizzle a little hempseed oil over the top and add some salt.

tapenade and yogurt ravioli with calaloo sauce

preparation: 20 minutes
cooking: 20 minutes
serves: 2

Calaloo is Caribbean spinach, available from West Indian grocers, usually in cans. If you can't find it, use fresh spinach instead.

1 To make the pasta, place the flours in a bowl and add the olive oil, soyannaise and salt and pepper. Mix with a fork, then knead gently until shiny and smooth. Wrap the dough in a plastic bag and chill until needed.

2 To make the sauce, heat the olive oil in a medium saucepan and fry the shallots until golden. Add the calaloo and stir until hot. Over a low heat, add the cream, a little at a time, then the bouillon powder, garlic, basil and salt and pepper. Stirring constantly, add the wine. Put a large saucepan of water on to boil.

3 Take the chilled dough, break it into 6 pieces and roll into balls. Flour a work surface and roll the balls into circles about 8 cm (3¼ inches) in diameter.

4 Cut each circle in half and spoon ½ teaspoon of tapenade and ½ teaspoon of yogurt slightly off-centre on each one. Fold the dough over to encase the filling and make a triangular shape, moisten the edges with a little soya milk, if you like, then press the edges together to seal.

5 Place the ravioli in the pan of boiling water and simmer for about 10 minutes, until hot. Drain and serve with the calaloo sauce, sprinkle with pepper and garnish with basil. A crisp green salad makes a good accompaniment.

Pasta
- **50 g (2 oz) semolina flour**
- **50 g (2 oz) strong white flour**
- **1 tablespoon olive oil**
- **1 tablespoon Soyannaise (see page 15)**
- **6 teaspoons vegan tapenade or pesto**
- **6 teaspoons Vegan Yogurt (see page 14)**
- **soya milk (optional)**
- **salt and pepper**

Calaloo sauce
- **1 tablespoon olive oil**
- **2 shallots, chopped**
- **275 g (9 oz) can calaloo, drained, or 250 g (8 oz) spinach, chopped**
- **6 tablespoons soya or coconut cream**
- **2 teaspoons vegan bouillon powder**
- **1 garlic clove, crushed**
- **4 basil leaves, chopped**
- **4 tablespoons dry white vegan wine, or half and half lemon juice and water**
- **salt and pepper**
- **basil leaves, to garnish**

- 125 g (4 oz) dried chestnuts
- 1.2 litres (2 pints) Vegetable
  Stock (see page 14)
- 750 g (1½ lb) potatoes, chopped
- 1 sweet potato, chopped
- 1 tablespoon olive oil
- 6 tomatoes, chopped
- 2 onions, chopped
- 1 carrot, chopped
- 125 g (4 oz) cauliflower,
  chopped
- 125 g (4 oz) frozen peas
- 1 green pepper, deseeded and
  chopped
- 1 small courgette, chopped
- 1 tablespoon chopped dates
- 1 tablespoon yeast extract
- 6 sprigs of rosemary, leaves
  only, finely chopped
- 3 tablespoons sweetened
  soya milk
- 1 tablespoon chopped parsley
- 1 heaped tablespoon cornflour
- 1 teaspoon carob powder
- 1 tablespoon balsamic vinegar
- 1 teaspoon blackstrap molasses
- 1 dessertspoon tomato purée
- 2 dessertspoons orange juice
- salt and pepper

chestnut cottage pies

A lovely winter warmer, this recipe uses individual pie dishes, but you could use one large pie dish if you prefer. The chestnuts absorb the flavours of the other ingredients, while adding their own nutty sweetness.

1 Cover the dried chestnuts with the stock and soak overnight, or boil them in the stock for 1 hour.

2 Place the potatoes and sweet potato in a pan of water, bring to the boil, then simmer until soft – about 25 minutes.

3 Meanwhile, heat the olive oil in a pan and add the tomatoes, all the remaining vegetables, the dates, yeast extract and rosemary. Add this mixture to the chestnuts and their liquid, much of which the chestnuts will have absorbed, and simmer for 15–20 minutes.

4 Preheat the oven to 180°C (350°F), Gas Mark 4. Drain the potatoes and mash them with the soya milk. Stir in the parsley, plus some salt and pepper.

5 Place the cornflour and carob powder in a small bowl, add the vinegar, molasses, tomato purée and orange juice and mix into a paste. Add the paste to the chestnut mixture, then stir over a low heat until the liquid thickens.

6 Divide the chestnut mixture equally between six 12 cm (5 inch) individual pie dishes. Place a layer of mashed potato on top. Bake for about 20 minutes, until lightly browned.

jamaican patties

Pastry

- 500 g (1 lb) plain flour
- 1 teaspoon baking powder
- 2 teaspoons curry powder
- ½ teaspoon salt
- 50 g (2 oz) coconut oil
- 50 ml (2 fl oz) rapeseed oil
- 125 ml (4 fl oz) cold rice milk or soya milk

Filling

- 25 g (1 oz) chilled, solidified coconut oil
- 75 g (3 oz) cassava, peeled and finely chopped
- 175 g (6 oz) sweet potato, finely chopped
- 1 red onion, finely chopped
- 125 g (4 oz) tofu, mashed
- 75 g (3 oz) chestnut mushrooms, finely chopped
- 50 g (2 oz) frozen peas
- 1 teaspoon chopped thyme
- 1 teaspoon curry powder
- ¼ teaspoon nutmeg
- salt and pepper

1 Place the flour, baking powder, curry powder and salt in a large bowl. Rub in the coconut oil, then stir in the rapeseed oil with a fork until the mixture resembles coarse breadcrumbs. Add just enough rice milk to make a dough that holds together. Wrap the dough in plastic bag and chill for at least 30 minutes.

2 To make the filling, heat the coconut oil in a large frying pan. Add the cassava and sweet potato and fry on a medium heat until they start to soften and brown. Add the onion and tofu and continue to cook, stirring, until they too start to brown. Stir in all the remaining ingredients, then cover and simmer for 5–10 minutes, until the sweet potato is cooked right through. Turn the mixture on to a plate and allow to cool.

3 Preheat the oven to 200°C (400°F), Gas Mark 6. Oil 2 baking sheets. Flour a work surface and roll out the chilled pastry to a thickness of 5 mm (¼ inch).

4 Cut twelve 10 cm (4 inch) circles out of the pastry. Spoon the filling equally on to the circles. Moisten the edges of the pastry with a little rice milk, then fold them over to make half-moon shapes and press the edges together with a fork.

5 Place the patties on the prepared baking sheets, brush with the remaining rice milk and prick the top of each patty with a fork. Bake for about 30 minutes, until the crust is golden brown. Serve with a rice salad or mashed potatoes and beans.

vegetable kebabs with satay sauce

preparation: 25 minutes
cooking: 30 minutes
serves: 4

These tasty kebabs can be grilled, baked or barbecued, but it's important to soak the kebab sticks first so that they don't burn.

1 Put 8 wooden satay or kebab sticks to soak in cold water for at least 20 minutes. Preheat the oven to 180°C (350°F), Gas Mark 4.

2 Pour the lime juice, molasses, soy sauce, chilli sauce and oil into a large bowl and mix well. Add the tofu and all the prepared fruit and vegetables, and stir until thoroughly coated.

3 Thread chunks of fruit and vegetables on to the soaked kebab sticks, alternating ingredients to give a range of colour and texture. Place on a baking sheet and bake for 30 minutes, or grill or barbecue until browned on all sides.

4 Meanwhile, prepare the sauce. Heat the oil in a medium pan, add the onion and fry gently until soft. Add the remaining sauce ingredients, stirring constantly until the peanut butter melts and the mixture is hot.

5 Serve the kebabs on a bed of brown basmati rice or stir-fried rice noodles with the satay sauce poured over the top. Garnish with a wedge of lime and a sprinkling of grated coconut and chopped coriander.

- 2 tablespoons lime juice
- 1 tablespoon blackstrap molasses
- 1 tablespoon soy sauce,
- 1 tablespoon sweet chilli sauce
- 1 tablespoon avocado oil
- 125 g (4 oz) tofu, cubed
- 1 tart apple, quartered
- 4 pineapple chunks
- 4 mango chunks
- 4 tomatoes, halved horizontally
- 1 red onion, quartered
- 8 mushrooms, halved
- 1 red and 1 green pepper, deseeded and quartered
- 1 sweetcorn cob, cooked and sliced into 8 rounds
- 1 sweet potato, boiled and thickly sliced
- 1 courgette, thickly sliced

Sauce
- 1 tablespoon coconut oil
- 1 onion, finely chopped
- 1 garlic clove, chopped
- 1 teaspoon ground cumin
- 125 g (4 oz) peanut butter
- 50 g (2 oz) creamed coconut
- 2 tablespoons lime juice
- 2 tablespoons soy sauce
- 2 tablespoons blackstrap molasses
- 3 tablespoons soya milk
- 1 tablespoon sweet chilli sauce

preparation: **15** minutes
cooking: **30** minutes
serves: **4**

- **2 medium potatoes, chopped**
- **1 lemon grass stalk**
- **4 tablespoons Puy lentils**
- **1 tablespoon coconut oil**
- **1 onion, chopped**
- **2 garlic cloves, chopped**
- **6 mushrooms, sliced**
- **1 teaspoon turmeric**
- **1 teaspoon ground cumin**
- **125 g (4 oz) green beans**
- **1 yellow pepper, deseeded and chopped**
- **1 courgette, chopped**
- **250 g (8 oz) frozen sweetcorn**
- **300 ml (½ pint) can coconut milk**
- **juice of 1 lime**
- **1 tablespoon chopped coriander leaves**

mild coconut curry

1 Put the potatoes, lemon grass and lentils into a medium saucepan and add enough boiling water to just cover the tops of the potatoes. Return to the boil, then simmer for about 15 minutes.

2 Heat the oil in a large saucepan and fry the onion, garlic, mushrooms, turmeric and cumin until the onion is soft. Add all the remaining ingredients, except for the coriander, and stir well.

3 Remove the lemon grass from the lentil pan, then add the lentil mixture to the onion mixture.

4 Simmer everything for about 10 minutes, or until the lentils are soft, then add the chopped coriander.

5 Serve with brown basmati rice cooked with a few cardamom pods, plus warm naan bread made without milk or yogurt.

wild mushroom and pine nut filo baskets

preparation: 15 minutes
cooking: 15 minutes
serves: 2

- 4 tablespoons avocado oil
- 1 red onion, chopped
- 375 g (12 oz) oyster mushrooms, stalks finely chopped, tops trimmed
- 50 g (2 oz) pine nuts
- 25 ml (1 fl oz) brandy or whisky
- 50 ml (2 fl oz) Vegetable Stock (see page 14)
- 1 tablespoon soy sauce
- 4 x 30 cm (12 inch) sheets of filo pastry
- 125 ml (4 fl oz) soya cream or Vegan Yogurt (see page 14)
- 1 tablespoon sweet chilli sauce, plus extra for drizzling
- 2 garlic cloves, chopped
- 1 tablespoon maple syrup (optional)
- 1 lime, sliced, to garnish (optional)

Try to find red oyster mushrooms for this recipe as they are full of flavour.

1 Preheat the oven to 180°C (350°F), Gas Mark 4. Heat 2 tablespoons of the oil in a medium saucepan and fry the onion, mushrooms, pine nuts and garlic until golden brown. Stir in the brandy, vegetable stock and soy sauce, then remove from the heat and set aside.

2 Take 1 sheet of filo pastry and lightly brush the surface with some of the remaining oil. Place another sheet on top and brush with oil. Cut the double thickness in half, place one half in a diamond shape over the square half below. This will make a star shape with 8 points.

3 Drape the prepared pastry over a small baking potato wrapped in foil. Brush the pastry with oil and place on a baking sheet. Repeat steps 2 and 3 until you have the basis of 4 filo baskets. Bake the filo baskets for about 10 minutes, until crisp and golden.

4 Stir 75 ml (3 fl oz) of the soya cream into the mushrooms, followed by the chilli sauce, garlic and maple syrup, if using. Return to a simmer.

5 Carefully lift the filo baskets from their supports, then fill with the mushroom mixture. Add drizzles of soya cream and sweet chilli sauce to each basket and garnish with a slice of lime, if you like. Serve with steamed mangetout and brown basmati rice.

- 4 ready-made corn tortillas
  (minus milk powder)

Filling
- 1 tablespoon olive oil
- 1 red onion, chopped
- 4 tablespoons soya mince
- 4 chestnut mushrooms, chopped
- 1 carrot, grated
- 125 g (4 oz) cooked kidney beans
- 125 g (4 oz) sweetcorn
- 1 tablespoon ground almonds
- 1 teaspoon chopped chilli
- ½ green pepper, deseeded and
  chopped
- 1 garlic clove, chopped
- 1 teaspoon each cumin, parsley
  and ground coriander
- 1 teaspoon yeast extract
- 250 ml (8 fl oz) Tomato and
  Orange Soup (see page 58)
- juice of ½ lime
- black pepper

Sauce
- 1 heaped tablespoon cornflour
- 2 tablespoons potato flour
- ½ teaspoon grated nutmeg
- 1 tablespoon vegan bouillon
  powder
- 1 tablespoon Dijon mustard
- 2 dessertspoons coconut oil
- 250 ml (8 fl oz) sweetened
  soya milk

enchiladas with mushroom and sweetcorn filling

1 Oil a roasting tin and preheat the oven to 200°C (400°F), Gas Mark 6.

2 To make the filling, heat the olive oil in a medium saucepan and fry the onion, mince and mushrooms for 5 minutes until soft. Stir in all the remaining filling ingredients with 100 ml (3½ fl oz) water and simmer for about 10 minutes.

3 Cook the tortillas according to the packet instructions and keep them warm while making the sauce, interleaving them with sheets of greaseproof paper so they don't stick together.

4 Place all the sauce ingredients in a small saucepan and heat until the mixture thickens.

5 Put 2 tablespoons of the filling on each tortilla, roll them up and put them in the prepared roasting tin. Spoon any remaining filling over the tortillas, then pour the sauce over them. Bake for 20 minutes until they start to bubble and brown.

6 Serve the enchiladas with a salad of red cabbage and red onions.

haggis and mashed root vegetables

Haggis
- **500 g (1 lb) swede, turnip or squash, finely chopped**
- **1 teaspoon finely chopped fresh root ginger**
- **50 g (2 oz) coconut oil**
- **125 g (4 oz) porridge oats**
- **1 onion, chopped**
- **4 mushrooms, chopped**
- **1 carrot, finely chopped**
- **200 g (7 oz) cooked kidney beans, chopped**
- **50 g (2 oz) shelled walnuts, chopped**
- **2 tablespoons rapeseed oil**
- **3 teaspoons yeast extract**
- **2 teaspoons black pepper**
- **½ teaspoon cayenne pepper**
- **1 teaspoon chopped parsley**
- **1 teaspoon chopped thyme**
- **1 teaspoon chopped sage**
- **½ teaspoon ground nutmeg**
- **2 tablespoons lime juice**
- **1 tablespoon soy sauce**
- **1 tablespoon whisky or balsamic vinegar**

Potato mash
- **625 g (1¼ lb) potatoes, quartered**
- **30 g (1¼ oz) vegan margarine**
- **1 tablespoon soya cream**
- **½ teaspoon chopped rosemary**
- **salt and pepper**

1 Preheat the oven to 180°C (350°F), Gas Mark 4. Place 375 g (12 oz) of the swede in a large saucepan of water, add the fresh root ginger, bring to the boil and simmer for 30 minutes. Put the potatoes for the mash in another large saucepan of cold water, bring to the boil and simmer for 30 minutes, until soft.

2 Meanwhile, heat 25 g (1 oz) of the coconut oil in a large nonstick frying pan and gently toast the oats for about 2 minutes, stirring constantly, until golden brown. Transfer to a bowl and set aside.

3 Heat the remaining coconut oil, then gently fry the remaining swede with the onion, mushrooms and carrot for about 10 minutes until the swede starts to soften. Add the kidney beans and stir until hot. Transfer the fried vegetables to the bowl of oats, then add all the remaining haggis ingredients.

4 Divide the mixture between four 8 cm (3¼ inch) ovenproof ramekins, cover with foil and place in a deep roasting tin half-filled with boiling water. Bake for 30 minutes.

5 Reheat the boiled swede, then drain and mash with half the margarine and salt and pepper. Reheat the boiled potatoes, then drain and mash with the soya cream, the remaining margarine and the rosemary.

6 Remove the ramekins from the oven, run a sharp knife round the edge of each one, then turn out on to warmed plates. Add 2 spoonfuls of each mash to the plates and serve this vegan version of the traditional Scottish sheep's sausage with a tot of whisky.

sunday roast drumsticks

preparation: **10** minutes
cooking: **30** minutes
serves: 2

The perfect choice for a festive dinner or a long, lazy Sunday lunch, these drumsticks are best served with rich gravy and red wine. Or, if you want an al fresco meal, press them around a wooden lolly stick and serve at a summer picnic.

1 Oil a baking sheet and preheat the oven to 200°C (400°F), Gas Mark 6. Place all the ingredients, apart from the coconut oil, in a bowl.

2 Melt the coconut oil and stir into the chestnut mixture to make a dough. Mould the dough into whatever shapes you like. (Drumsticks are good for Sunday lunch or picnics.)

3 Place the shapes on the prepared baking sheet and bake for 30 minutes, turning once.

4 Serve the drumsticks with roast potatoes, broccoli drizzled with hemp oil, carrots cooked in orange juice, steamed Brussels sprouts and cranberry sauce.

- 3 tablespoons dried TVP rehydrated in 125 ml (4 fl oz) hot Vegetable Stock (see page 14), or 3 heaped tablespoons crumbled smoked tofu
- 3 tablespoons dry sage and onion stuffing mix
- 250 g (8 oz) can chestnuts, drained and mashed
- 425 g (14 oz) can butter beans, drained and mashed
- 1 dessertspoon herbes de Provence
- juice of ½ lime
- 2 heaped tablespoons coconut oil
- salt and pepper

- **1.5 litres (2½ pints) Vegetable Stock (see page 14)**
- **pinch of saffron threads**
- **2 bay leaves**
- **25 g (1 oz) dried porcini mushrooms, broken into pieces**
- **2 dessertspoons dried arame seaweed, crushed**
- **3 teaspoons vegan bouillon powder**
- **1 tablespoon avocado oil**
- **2 tablespoons coconut oil**
- **1 small onion, finely chopped**
- **2 garlic cloves, finely chopped**
- **375 g (12 oz) risotto rice**
- **500 ml (17 fl oz) dry white wine**
- **50 g (2 oz) toasted pine nuts**
- **125 g (4 oz) frozen peas**
- **4 tablespoons ground almonds**
- **1 tablespoon chopped basil**
- **salt and pepper**
- **hemp oil, to serve**

arame almond risotto

1   Pour the vegetable stock into a large saucepan, bring to the boil, then reduce to a simmer. Add the saffron, bay leaves, mushrooms, arame and 1 teaspoon of the bouillon powder, stir and leave to simmer.

2   Heat the avocado oil and 1 tablespoon of the coconut oil in a large frying pan, add the onion and garlic and fry gently until translucent. Pour the rice into the pan and fry for about 5 minutes without browning.

3   When the rice is crackling hot, add 1 ladleful of hot stock and stir for 2–3 minutes. When the rice has absorbed that liquid, add 1½ ladlefuls of stock and stir again until absorbed.

4   Add the wine, a glass at a time, and continue stirring and cooking the risotto over a low heat. When a spoon drawn through the rice leaves a clear, dry wake behind it, add more stock.

5   When the risotto is thoroughly cooked – the rice grains should be firm to the bite, neither mushy nor chalky, and the texture creamy – stir in the remaining coconut oil plus the pine nuts, peas and salt and pepper.

6   Remove the bay leaves from the stock, then pour the stock, plus the arame and mushrooms, into the rice. Take the rice off the heat, stir thoroughly, then cover and leave to stand for 5 minutes.

7   Gently warm the ground almonds in a hot oven for a few minutes, then mix with the remaining bouillon powder. Stir the basil into the risotto, then transfer to a warmed serving dish. Sprinkle with the ground almonds, a few twists of black pepper and a drizzle of hemp oil.

pumpkin pie

- 2 tablespoons olive oil
- 1 small pumpkin or squash, deseeded and chopped
- 2 small onions, chopped
- 1 teaspoon turmeric
- 1 teaspoon paprika
- 1 teaspoon cinnamon
- 2 carrots, grated
- ½ red pepper, deseeded and chopped
- 25 g (1 oz) stoned prunes, chopped
- 1 tablespoon blackstrap molasses
- rind and juice of 1 orange
- 500 g (1 lb) vegan shortcrust pastry
- 25 g (1 oz) ground almonds
- 25 g (1 oz) ground pumpkin seeds
- 125 ml (4 fl oz) soya milk
- 125 ml (4 fl oz) rapeseed oil
- juice of 1 lime
- 1 tablespoon Dijon mustard

Like many squashes, pumpkin has a subtle flavour, so it can be mixed with a variety of other ingredients to make both sweet and savoury dishes.

1 Oil a 30 cm (12 inch) pie dish. Preheat the oven to 200°C (400°F), Gas Mark 6. Heat 1 tablespoon of the olive oil in a large saucepan and gently fry the pumpkin, onions, turmeric, paprika and cinnamon until the pumpkin is soft. Add the carrots, red pepper, prunes, molasses and orange rind and juice, stir until hot, then remove from the heat.

2 Roll out the pastry on a floured surface and use to line the prepared pie dish. Reserve the trimmings.

3 Mix the ground almonds and pumpkin seeds and sprinkle them on the pastry base. Spread the pumpkin mixture on top of the seed mixture.

4 Heat the soya milk until almost boiling, then add the rapeseed oil, mixing well with a hand-held blender. With the blender running, gradually add the lime juice, then the mustard. Spread the mixture on top of the pie.

5 Roll out the pastry trimmings on a floured surface and cut into strips 1 cm (½ inch) wide. Weave them on top of the pie to create a lattice effect. Brush the pastry with the remaining olive oil and bake the pie for 30 minutes.

6 Serve the pie hot with baked beans and mashed potato and a green salad.

sea-fruit strudel

preparation: **20** minutes

cooking: **40** minutes

serves: **6**

1 Preheat the oven to 200°C (400°F), Gas Mark 6. Place the seaweed in a bowl and sprinkle with the lime juice. Lightly brush the filo sheets with avocado oil and arrange in 2 piles on sheets of greaseproof paper at least 5 cm (2 inches) bigger all round.

2 Heat 2 tablespoons of the avocado oil in a large nonstick frying pan and gently fry the onion, aubergine, mushrooms and mustard seeds. Add the red pepper and the seaweed with the lime juice and simmer until all the juices have been absorbed. Remove from the heat and mix in the remaining ingredients.

3 Divide the mixture equally between the 2 piles of filo, spreading it evenly over the surface and leaving a 3 cm (1½ inch) gap along the edge furthest from you.

4 Using the greaseproof paper, gently roll the pastry into a log shape and press along the empty edge to seal. With the strudels still sitting on the paper, gently lift them on to a baking sheet, ensuring that the seal is underneath. You might have to bend them to fit, but that gives a nice wrinkled effect.

5 Cut off the excess paper, then brush the strudels with the remaining oil and sprinkle with sesame seeds. Bake for 30 minutes until crisp and golden. When ready, cut into slices and serve with a spicy rice salad and curly kale tossed in oil and crushed garlic.

- **25 g (1 oz) mixed Atlantic seaweed**
- **juice of 2 limes**
- **500 g (1 lb) packet filo pastry (large sheets)**
- **5 tablespoons avocado oil**
- **1 red onion, chopped**
- **1 small aubergine, chopped**
- **50 g (2 oz) mushrooms, chopped**
- **1 teaspoon brown mustard seeds**
- **½ red pepper, deseeded and chopped**
- **50 g (2 oz) dried apricots, chopped**
- **50 g (2 oz) chopped hazelnuts**
- **50 g (2 oz) pine nuts**
- **1 tablespoon capers**
- **rind of 1 orange**
- **1 tablespoon miso**
- **½ teaspoon cayenne pepper**
- **1 tart apple, cored and chopped**
- **black pepper**
- **1 tablespoon sesame seeds, to garnish**

Quenelles

- 125 g (4 oz) brown basmati rice
- 50 g (2 oz) wild rice
- 125 g (4 oz) Puy lentils
- 600 ml (1 pint) Vegetable Stock (see page 14)
- 50 g (2 oz) self-raising wholemeal flour
- 1 tablespoon desiccated coconut
- 1 dessertspoon dried seaweed flakes
- 1 garlic clove, finely chopped
- 1 teaspoon cumin
- 1 teaspoon chopped mint
- 50 g (2 oz) coconut oil

Tomato sauce

- 1 tablespoon olive oil
- 1 red onion, chopped
- 1 red pepper, deseeded and chopped
- 1 small red chilli, finely chopped (optional)
- 4 tomatoes, chopped
- 1 tablespoon arrowroot
- juice of ½ lime
- 1 tablespoon blackstrap molasses
- 1 tablespoon balsamic vinegar
- 1 teaspoon salt
- black pepper, to taste

wild rice and lentil quenelles in tomato sauce

1 Place the rice and lentils in a large saucepan, add 600 ml (1 pint) of water, bring to the boil and simmer for 5 minutes. Drain, rinse well, then return the rice and lentils to the pan.

2 Add the vegetable stock, bring to the boil and simmer for 15–20 minutes, until the rice is cooked.

3 Meanwhile, make the sauce. Heat the olive oil in a small saucepan and gently fry the onion until soft. Add the red pepper, chilli and tomatoes to the pan and simmer for about 10 minutes.

4 Oil a baking sheet and preheat the oven to 180°C (350°F), Gas Mark 4. Drain the rice and lentils, place in a mixing bowl and add the flour, coconut, seaweed, garlic, cumin, mint and salt and pepper.

5 Using 2 dessertspoons dipped in warm water to prevent sticking, shape the lentil mixture into ovals the size of an egg and place them on the prepared baking sheet. Top each quenelle with a knob of coconut oil and bake for about 20 minutes, turning and basting occasionally, until golden and crispy all over.

6 Place the tomato mixture in a food processor or liquidizer and blend until smooth. Mix together the arrowroot and lime juice and add to the sauce. With the machine still running, add the molasses, vinegar and salt and pepper, then return the sauce to the pan and simmer until the mixture thickens.

7 To serve, put the crispy quenelles into warmed bowls and pour over the tomato sauce. A crisp green side salad makes a good accompaniment.

preparation: 10 minutes
cooking: 10 minutes
serves: 2

rice noodle and vegetable stir-fry

- 50 g (2 oz) rice noodles
- 1 dessertspoon coconut oil
- 1 red onion, sliced
- 250 g (8 oz) rehydrated soya chunks or tofu
- 2 tablespoons soy sauce
- 1 teaspoon finely chopped fresh root ginger
- 1 garlic clove, finely chopped
- 125 g (4 oz) cabbage, finely sliced
- 125 g (4 oz) bean sprouts
- 8 lychees, peeled, stoned and quartered
- 1 dessertspoon blackstrap molasses

To serve
- nori flakes
- sesame seeds
- lime wedges (optional)

1 Soak the rice noodles in boiling water for 4 minutes, then rinse in cold water and drain.

2 Heat a wok or large frying pan until very hot, add the coconut oil, then the onion and soya. Stir briskly to sear on all sides until golden.

3 Pour in the soy sauce and stir to coat the mixture.

4 Reduce the heat and add the remaining ingredients plus the drained noodles, stirring until hot.

5 Transfer the stir-fry to warmed serving bowls, sprinkle with the nori flakes and sesame seeds, and serve with a wedges of lime, if liked.

spicy basmati salad

- **250 g (8 oz) brown basmati rice, rinsed**
- **125 g (4 oz) Puy lentils, rinsed**
- **1 litre (1¾ pints) Vegetable Stock (see page 14)**
- **2 tablespoons olive oil**
- **2 small onions, chopped**
- **4 garlic cloves, minced**
- **6 chestnut mushrooms, finely chopped**
- **2 tablespoons curry paste**
- **150 ml (¼ pint) apple juice**
- **juice of 1 lime**
- **1 teaspoon vegan bouillon powder**
- **2 dessertspoons sultanas**
- **1 dessertspoon mango chutney**
- **75 g (3 oz) sweetcorn**
- **1 red pepper, deseeded and finely chopped**
- **2 tomatoes, finely chopped**
- **coconut flakes and sprigs of coriander, to serve**

1 Place the rice, lentils and vegetable stock in a saucepan, bring to the boil and simmer for 20 minutes, until almost cooked.

2 Meanwhile, heat the olive oil in a large saucepan and gently fry the onions until soft. Add the garlic and mushrooms and cook until soft.

3 Stir in the curry paste and heat through. Add the apple and lime juices, bouillon powder, sultanas and chutney, stir well and simmer for 3 minutes.

4 Drain the rice and lentils and add to the curry mixture. Stir in the sweetcorn, red pepper and tomatoes, then simmer for 10 minutes until the juices are absorbed and the rice is completely tender.

5 Serve sprinkled with coconut flakes and sprigs of coriander. Roasted Vegetables (see page 48) and a mixed salad are good accompaniments.

walnut and mushroom pie

preparation: 20 minutes
cooking: 40–45 minutes
serves: 6

When stewed in gravy, walnuts develop a velvety richness. They are reputed to be good for the kidneys, lubricating the digestive system and improving the metabolism.

1 Oil a 30 cm (12 inch) pie dish or six 10 cm (4 inch) individual dishes. Preheat the oven to 180°C (350°F) Gas Mark 4.

2 Place the tomatoes in a food processor or liquidizer and blend to a purée. Transfer the purée to a large saucepan and bring to the boil, then reduce the heat to a simmer. Add the mushrooms, walnuts, carrot, onion, red pepper, dates and mustard powder, stir well, then cover the pan and simmer for 15 minutes.

3 Meanwhile, flour a work surface, cut the pastry in half and roll out to a 5 mm (¼ inch) thickness. Use to line the prepared dish or dishes, arrange baking parchment over the pastry and place some baking beans on top, then bake blind for 7 minutes.

4 Combine all the remaining ingredients in a small jug and gradually pour into the stew, stirring constantly as it thickens.

5 Spoon the stew into the pie crust. Roll out the remaining pastry and use to cover the pie(s).

6 Brush the pastry with soyannaise, sprinkle with the sesame seeds and bake the pie(s) for 25–30 minutes, until puffed and golden. Serve with mashed potato and steamed vegetables drizzled with oil.

- 250 g (8 oz) can tomatoes
- 375 g (12 oz) oyster mushrooms, sliced
- 125 g (4 oz) shelled walnuts
- 1 carrot, finely chopped
- 1 red onion, chopped
- 1 red pepper, deseeded and chopped
- 1 tablespoon chopped dates
- 1 teaspoon mustard powder
- 500 g (1 lb) vegan puff pastry
- 1 tablespoon vegan gravy powder or cornflour
- 1 teaspoon carob powder
- 2 tablespoons rapeseed oil
- 1 dessertspoon yeast extract
- 1 tablespoon balsamic vinegar
- 1 tablespoon chopped parsley
- 1 teaspoon black pepper
- 1 tablespoon Soyannaise (see page 15), to glaze
- 1 dessertspoon sesame seeds, to garnish

mushroom stew with herb dumplings

- 1 potato, chopped
- 25 g (1 oz) dried shiitake mushrooms, broken into pieces
- 125 g (4 oz) Puy lentils
- 600 ml (1 pint) Vegetable Stock (see page 14)
- 125 g (4 oz) oyster mushrooms, sliced
- 1 red onion, chopped
- 1 carrot, chopped
- 125 g (4 oz) frozen peas
- 1 red pepper, deseeded and chopped
- 125 g (4 oz) cabbage, chopped
- 2 heaped teaspoons cornflour
- 2 teaspoons carob powder
- 2 teaspoons vegan bouillon powder
- 1 tablespoon molasses
- 1 teaspoon yeast extract
- 2 tablespoons vegan tomato sauce
- 125 ml (4 fl oz) vegan sherry

Dumplings

- 175 g (6 oz) self-raising wholemeal flour
- 1 teaspoon vegan bouillon powder
- 1 teaspoon chopped sage
- 1 teaspoon chopped thyme
- 1 teaspoon chopped parsley
- 50 ml (2 fl oz) rapeseed oil
- 125 ml (4 fl oz) soya milk

1 Place the potato, shiitake mushrooms and lentils in a large saucepan, add the stock and 200 ml (7 fl oz) water and bring to the boil. Reduce the heat and simmer for 20 minutes.

2 Put all the dumpling ingredients in a food processor, mix well, then divide the mixture into 12 balls.

3 Add the remaining vegetables to the potato mixture.

4 Place the cornflour, carob powder and bouillon powder in a mixing bowl, add the molasses, yeast extract, tomato sauce and sherry, and stir until smooth. Gradually add this mixture to the vegetables, stirring constantly as the stew thickens.

5 Sit the dumplings on the stew, replace the lid and simmer gently for about another 20 minutes, until the dumplings are cooked. (If you prefer, you can cook the stew and dumplings in a casserole dish, covered, in a preheated oven at 180°C (350°F), Gas Mark 4.)

- 150 g (5 oz) millet
- 500 ml (17 fl oz) Vegetable Stock (see page 14)
- 10 cm (4 inch) piece of lemon grass
- 1 slice of fresh root ginger
- 2 tablespoons olive oil
- 1 red onion, chopped
- 50 g (2 oz) pumpkin seeds, ground
- 1 carrot, grated
- 1 garlic clove, chopped
- 15 g (½ oz) dried shiitake mushrooms, ground (use a herb mill or a coffee grinder)
- 1 dessertspoon carob powder
- 2 teaspoons chopped thyme
- 1 dessertspoon balsamic vinegar
- 1 dessertspoon soy sauce
- 1 teaspoon yeast extract
- 1 tablespoon coconut oil, for greasing
- salt and pepper

millet burgers

These succulent burgers can be served in the traditional way or allowed to become cold, then marinated in a mixture of soy sauce and olive oil with a dash of balsamic vinegar and barbecued. They can also be used cold in sandwiches with pickles or put into pitta bread with some crisp salad and chilli sauce.

1 Preheat the oven to 180°C (350°F), Gas Mark 4. Place the millet in a saucepan, add the stock and bring to the boil. Reduce the heat, add the lemon grass and ginger, and simmer for about 30 minutes, until the liquid has been absorbed.

2 Meanwhile, heat the olive oil in a frying pan and gently fry the onion until beginning to brown.

3 Once the millet is cooked, discard the ginger and lemon grass, then add the onion and all the remaining ingredients.

4 Grease a baking sheet with the coconut oil, then put spoonfuls of the millet mixture on it, flattening them out to about 7 cm (3 inches) in diameter and 1.5 cm (½ inch) thick.

5 Bake the burgers for about 40 minutes, turning them halfway through. They should be firm and succulent. Serve in buns with sauerkraut and a crisp green salad.

chapter four
desserts

preparation: 15 minutes
cooking: 25–35 minutes
serves: 8–10 brownies

date and prune brownies

- 250 g (8 oz) wholemeal flour
- 250 ml (8 fl oz) rice milk or water
- 50 ml (2 fl oz) soya milk
- 50 ml (2 fl oz) rapeseed oil
- 3 tablespoons cocoa powder
- 1 tablespoon carob powder
- 250 g (8 oz) dark brown sugar
- 1 teaspoon salt
- 1 teaspoon vanilla essence
- 125 g (4 oz) ready-to-eat dried prunes, stoned
- 50 g (2 oz) medjool dates, stoned
- 1½ teaspoons baking powder
- 1 tablespoon ground almonds

1 Line a 27 x 17 x 3.5 cm (10½ x 6½ x 1½ inch) baking tin with baking parchment and oil lightly. Preheat the oven to 180°C (350°F), Gas Mark 4.

2 Place 2 heaped tablespoons of the flour in a saucepan and mix in the rice milk. Cook, stirring constantly, over a medium heat until thick. Set aside to cool completely.

3 Combine the soya milk, oil, cocoa and carob in a bowl and stir until smooth.

4 Transfer the cooled flour mixture to a food processer or liquidizer, add the sugar, salt, vanilla, prunes and dates, and blend until smooth. Add the cocoa mixture and blend again.

5 Mix the remaining flour with the baking powder and the ground almonds, then add to the prune mixture and blend again. Pour the mixture into the prepared tin and bake for 25–35 minutes, until firm to the touch.

6 Cut into slices and serve hot with a scoop of vegan ice cream and some grated chocolate.

preparation: 10 minutes
cooking: 23 minutes
serves: 6

lime soufflettes

- 2 limes
- 250 ml (8 fl oz) sweetened soya milk
- 4 heaped tablespoons icing sugar
- 250 ml (8 fl oz) rapeseed oil
- slices of lime, to decorate (optional)

This vegan recipe is, of course, made without eggs or cream, so to call it a soufflé would be regarded as culinary treason in some parts of the world. However, as it's so creamy and zesty it would be a great shame to go through life without enjoying a spoonful.

1 Preheat the oven to 200°C (400°F), Gas Mark 6. Pare the rind from one of the limes and squeeze the juice from both.

2 Heat the soya milk with the sugar until hot but not boiling. Transfer the mixture to a food processor or liquidizer, add the oil and blend briefly. Gradually add the lime juice, whisking constantly to avoid curdling.

3 Stir in the lime rind, then pour the mixture into six 8 cm (3¼ inch) ramekins and bake for 20 minutes until the soufflettes have risen just above the rims of the ramekins.

4 Allow to cool, then serve with strawberries or slices of mango and some curls of vegan ice cream. Decorate with slices of lime, if you like.

moist chocolate crumb cake

preparation: 15 minutes, plus cooling
cooking: 45 minutes
serves: 8

1 Preheat the oven to 180°C (350°F), Gas Mark 4. Crush the biscuits, then pour them into a small saucepan and heat gently with the coconut oil and soya milk for a few minutes, stirring, until well combined.

2 Using the back of a spoon, press the crumb mixture into the bottom of a 30 cm (12 inch) flan dish or into eight 8 cm (3¼ inch) ramekins.

3 Place all the remaining ingredients in a bowl and combine with a hand-held mixer or blender.

4 Pour the tofu mixture on top of the biscuit base, then bake for 45 minutes. Allow to cool for 2 hours before serving.

5 Decorate with crystallized ginger and nasturtium leaves, then serve with a spoonful of ice cream and a drizzle of maple syrup.

- 12 vegan digestives, gingernuts, bourbons or oat biscuits
- 25 g (1 oz) coconut oil
- 25 ml (1 fl oz) soya milk
- 250 g (8 oz) silken tofu
- 2 teaspoons arrowroot
- 1 banana
- 4 tablespoons cocoa powder
- 150 ml (¼ pint) maple syrup
- 2 tablespoons tahini
- 2 tablespoons raisins
- 1 tablespoon lime juice
- 3 tablespoons orange juice
- 2 teaspoons vanilla essence
- pinch of salt

To decorate
- crystallized ginger
- nasturtium leaves

- 100 g (3½ oz) dairy-free dark chocolate (70 per cent cocoa solids)
- 1 tablespoon chopped walnuts
- 200 ml (7 fl oz) coconut cream
- 2 tablespoons mixed dried fruit
- 50 g (2 oz) dates, chopped
- 50 g (2 oz) ready-to-eat dried apricots, chopped
- 1 tablespoon Cointreau
- 2 tablespoons agave or maple syrup
- 2 tablespoons lime juice
- 2 tablespoons Essential Seed Mix (see page 20)
- 2 tablespoons flax oil
- 2 tablespoons porridge oats
- 100 ml (3½ fl oz) soya milk
- 2 teaspoons carob powder
- 1 tablespoon Vegan Yogurt (see page 14)
- 1 tablespoon vegan margarine

chocolate chip and walnut ice cream

Is there a more delicious way of getting your daily dose of essential omega 3 than a portion of this soft-set ice cream? We don't think so. Try it with Chocolate Chip Cookies (see page 124).

1 Break the chocolate into pieces, then place 75 g (3 oz) of it in a heatproof bowl over a saucepan of simmering water and heat until melted. (Do not let the bowl touch the water.)

2 Chop the remaining chocolate into chip-sized pieces, mix with the walnuts and set aside.

3 Place all the remaining ingredients in a bowl and use a hand-held mixer to combine until quite smooth. Stir the melted chocolate into the fruit mixture, then mix in the walnuts and chocolate chips.

4 Transfer the mixture to a suitable lidded container and place in the freezer for 1 hour. Remove from the freezer and break up the mixture with a fork to reduce the ice crystals. Repeat this process every hour for the next 4 hours.

5 If frozen for longer than 24 hours, remove the ice cream from the freezer 15 minutes before you want to serve it. Serve with drizzles of soya cream, maple syrup, a sprinkle of cinnamon and some fruit of your choice.

chocolate mousse with banana cake hearts

Mousse
- 175 g (6 oz) dairy-free chocolate (70 per cent cocoa solids)
- 50 g (2 oz) coconut oil
- 50 ml (2 fl oz) orange juice
- 50 g (2 oz) dark brown sugar
- 125 ml (4 fl oz) sunflower oil
- 125 ml (4 fl oz) sweetened soya milk
- 50 g (2 oz) medjool dates, stoned and chopped
- 2 tablespoons Cointreau

Banana cake
- 1 banana, mashed
- 125 g (4 oz) self-raising wholemeal flour
- 50 ml (2 fl oz) rapeseed oil
- 50 ml (2 fl oz) soya milk
- 50 ml (2 fl oz) agave or maple syrup
- 1 tablespoon chopped glacé cherries
- 1 teaspoon finely grated lemon rind
- 1 teaspoon lemon juice

To decorate
- soya cream
- grated chocolate

Good dairy-free dark chocolate is essential for this recipe.

1 Break the chocolate into pieces, place in a saucepan with the coconut oil, orange juice and sugar, and melt over a low heat, stirring constantly.

2 Place the sunflower oil and soya milk in a bowl and combine thoroughly using a hand-held mixer. With the mixer still running, gradually add the melted chocolate mixture. Stir in the dates and Cointreau, then chill the mousse in the refrigerator for at least 2 hours.

3 Meanwhile, make the banana cake. Oil a 20 cm (8 inch) cake tin. Preheat the oven to 180°C (350°F), Gas Mark 4.

4 Place all the cake ingredients in a bowl and mix thoroughly. Pour the mixture into the prepared cake tin and bake for 20–25 minutes, or until the tip of a sharp knife inserted in the middle of the cake comes out clean.

5 Allow the cake to cool, then use a heart-shaped cutter to cut out 12 heart shapes from the cake.

6 Whisk the mousse again, then spoon into ramekins or glass dishes. Place a cake heart on top of each one. Drizzle each serving with soya cream and sprinkle with coarsely grated chocolate.

flaming hot peaches with chocolate sauce

preparation: 15 minutes
cooking: 10 minutes
serves: 2

This dessert is a real show-stopper. The flaming is most impressive if done at the table with the lights down low.

1 Place the cream cheese in a bowl and mash 2 of the strawberries into it.

2 Cut a sliver of flesh from the curved side of each peach half so that they sit level on a plate. Spoon the cream cheese mixture into the hollows of the peaches. Chill in the refrigerator while you make the sauce.

3 Break the chocolate into pieces and melt in a bowl placed over a saucepan of simmering water. (Do not let the bowl touch the water.)

4 Mix in the agave syrup, then add the soya cream or soya milk, a little at a time. Stir in the Cointreau, if using.

5 Decorate the peaches with grated chocolate and with the remaining strawberries, sliced into fans (see page 28, step 3).

6 Heat the whisky in a small saucepan on the stove or a jug in the microwave. When hot, but not boiling, set alight and carefully pour the flaming liquid over the cold peaches and watch the chocolate melt.

- 2 tablespoons Vegan Cream Cheese (see page 14)
- 6 strawberries
- 2 peaches, halved and stoned
- 25 g (1 oz) dairy-free dark chocolate (70 per cent cocoa solids), coarsely grated or finely chopped
- 4 tablespoons whisky or brandy

Chocolate sauce
- 75 g (3 oz) dairy-free dark chocolate (70 per cent cocoa solids)
- 1 tablespoon agave syrup
- 250 ml (8 fl oz) carton of soya cream, or 175 ml (6 fl oz) sweetened soya milk
- 1 tablespoon Cointreau (optional)

preparation: 15 minutes
cooking: 25–30 minutes
serves: 8

Cake

- 250 g (8 oz) self-raising wholemeal flour
- 250 g (8 oz) soft brown sugar
- 2 tablespoons cocoa powder
- 2 heaped teaspoons carob powder
- 125 ml (4 fl oz) rapeseed oil
- 150 ml (¼ pint) soya milk
- 1 tablespoon Vegan Yogurt (see page 14), bean curd or coconut cream
- 1 dessertspoon cider vinegar
- pinch of salt
- 25 g (1 oz) dairy-free dark chocolate (70 per cent cocoa solids)
- fresh cherries or berries, to decorate

Filling

- 4 tablespoons Vegan Cream Cheese (see page 14)
- 1 teaspoon lime rind
- 4 tablespoons morello cherry or blackberry jam

black forest chocolate cake

You don't need eggs to make a light-as-air sponge cake. This dairy-free version of a classic gâteau shows you how.

1 Oil two 20 cm (8 inch) circular sponge tins and line them with baking parchment. Preheat the oven to 180°C (350°F), Gas Mark 4.

2 Place all the cake ingredients, except the chocolate, in a food processor and beat together thoroughly.

3 Coarsely grate or chop the chocolate and add to the cake mixture. Divide the mixture between the sponge tins and level the tops with a spatula.

4 Bake for 25–30 minutes, or until a cocktail stick inserted into the centre of each sponge comes out clean. Allow to cool a little, then turn out on to a wire rack to become completely cold.

5 Place the cream cheese in a bowl and stir in the lime rind. Spread one side of a cold sponge with the lime cream cheese, and spread the other sponge with jam. Sandwich together and put on a serving plate.

6 Decorate the cake with fresh cherries or berries and serve with vanilla ice cream and hot Chocolate Sauce (see page 113) made with Kirsch rather than Cointreau.

mango ice cream

- 2 large mangoes, skinned, stoned and chopped
- 75 g (3 oz) ready-to-eat dried apricots, chopped
- 1 banana
- 3 tablespoons sunflower oil
- 1 tablespoon flax oil
- 1 tablespoon soya lecithin
- 4 tablespoons soya milk
- 125 g (4 oz) Essential Seed Mix (see page 20)
- 1 tablespoon lime juice

This exotic fruity ice cream is nutritious as well as delicious. It also makes an excellent base for a smoothie (see page 21).

1 Place the mangoes, apricots and banana in a liquidizer and blend to a smooth consistency.

2 Combine the oils, soya lecithin and soya milk and whisk well. Add the blended fruit and whisk again. Stir in the seed mix.

3 Transfer the ice-cream mixture to a shallow container with an airtight lid and freeze for 1 hour. Remove from the freezer and break up the mixture with a fork to reduce the ice crystals. Repeat this process every hour for the next 4 hours.

4 Serve the ice cream with berries and coconut cream.

pecan pie

preparation: **15** minutes
cooking: **35** minutes
serves: **6**

Pecan trees are grown mainly in North America, where the nuts were an important food source for native Americans. In the recent years, they have been used mostly in ice creams, confectionery and sweet pastries, such as this one. The addition of molasses adds a rich dark taste and texture, as well as a good helping of calcium, and is balanced by the hint of cinnamon.

- 250 g (8 oz) vegan shortcrust pastry
- 2 tablespoons self-raising unbleached flour
- 2 tablespoons blackstrap molasses
- 175 ml (6 fl oz) maple syrup
- 1 teaspoon carob powder
- ½ teaspoon ground cinnamon
- 75 g (3 oz) pecans, finely chopped
- 75 ml (3 fl oz) soya milk
- 75 ml (3 fl oz) rapeseed oil
- 1 dessertspoon lime juice
- 75 g (3 oz) whole pecans

1 Preheat the oven to 180°C (350°F), Gas Mark 4. Oil a 25 cm (10 inch) pie dish.

2 On a floured surface, roll out the pastry and use it to line the pie dish, trimming off any excess. Arrange baking parchment on top of the pastry, place baking beans on top and bake blind for 10 minutes.

3 Place the flour, molasses, maple syrup, carob powder, cinnamon and chopped pecans in a bowl and mix well.

4 Heat the soya milk until almost boiling, add the rapeseed oil and mix well using an electric whisk. Continue whisking as you add the lime juice.

5 Fold this liquid into the maple syrup mixture, then pour into the pie case. Arrange the whole pecans on top and bake for 20 minutes.

6 Serve warm with vegan ice cream or soya cream and maple syrup.

peach, apricot and fig crumble with custard

Crumble

- 125 g (4 oz) plain wholemeal flour
- 2 tablespoons rapeseed oil
- 2 tablespoons sweetened soya milk
- 25 g (1 oz) porridge oats
- 50 g (2 oz) dark brown sugar
- 25 g (1 oz) flaked almonds
- 250 g (8 oz) peaches, stoned and sliced
- 250 g (8 oz) ready-to-eat dried apricots, chopped
- 6 fresh or dried figs, diced
- juice of 1 lime
- ¼ teaspoon ground nutmeg
- 1 teaspoon ground cinnamon

Custard

- 2 tablespoons custard powder or cornflour
- 3 tablespoons maple syrup
- 600 ml (1 pint) oat milk or soya milk

Crumbles are comfort food, best eaten with custard, but are also delicious with ice cream or soya cream. The fruit content can be varied in any way you like: try plum and ginger, strawberry and mango, pear and prunes, apple and raspberry, or banana, pineapple and coconut.

1 Preheat the oven to 180°C (350°F), Gas Mark 4. Pour the flour into a large bowl and lightly mix in the oil and the soya milk with a fork until the mixture forms coarse crumbs. Stir the oats, sugar and flaked almonds into the mixture.

2 Place the fruit in a 1.2 litre (2 pint) ovenproof dish and sprinkle it with about 4 tablespoons water, the lime juice, nutmeg and cinnamon.

3 Spoon the crumble mixture over the fruit and bake for 25–30 minutes, until golden brown.

4 Put the custard powder in a jug, add the maple syrup and 4 tablespoons of the oat milk and stir together well.

5 Heat the remaining milk in a small saucepan until hot but not boiling, then remove from the heat and gradually stir in the custard powder mixture to thicken. Return the pan to a medium heat and cook for a few minutes, stirring constantly.

6 Serve the crumble with the hot custard.

- 150 g (5 oz) ready-to-eat dried apricots, chopped
- 25 g (1 oz) dried papaya, chopped
- 450 ml (¾ pint) sweetened soya milk
- 2 tablespoons flax oil
- 6 strawberries or 1 kiwi fruit, to decorate

apricot and papaya fool

A light and luscious dessert, much healthier than the non-vegan version, which has lashings of whipped cream.

1 Soak the dried apricots and papaya in the soya milk overnight.

2 Transfer the dried fruit and soya milk to a food processor or liquidizer and blend to a smooth consistency. Add the oil and blend again.

3 Divide the mixture between 6 small glass dishes, then refrigerate until set.

4 Decorate each serving with a sliced strawberry fan (see page 28, step 3) or some slivers of kiwi fruit. Serve with coconut cream.

crème caramel

preparation: 10 minutes, plus chilling
cooking: 25 minutes
serves: 6

The classic French recipe for this dessert is totally dependent on dairy produce. This version tastes equally good with none at all.

1 Thoroughly oil six 8 cm (3¼ inch) ovenproof ramekins. Preheat the oven to 180°C (350°F), Gas Mark 4.

2 Stir the sugar into the soya milk, then heat until hot but not boiling. Transfer to a food processor or liquidizer. Add the oil and mix well. Keep the machine running as you add the vanilla essence and 1 tablespoon of the lime juice. The mixture will thicken slightly.

3 Add the cornflour and mix again. Add the molasses and the remaining lime juice and mix once more. Divide the mixture between the ramekins, place on a baking tray and bake for 25 minutes.

4 Allow to cool, then refrigerate for 2 hours.

5 To serve, stand the ramekins in hot water for a few minutes, then carefully run a very sharp, thin knife round the edges. Turn out on to small plates, drizzle with a little molasses and decorate with strawberries dusted with icing sugar.

- 4 heaped tablespoons icing sugar
- 250 ml (8 fl oz) sweetened soya milk
- 250 ml (8 fl oz) rapeseed oil
- 2 teaspoons vanilla essence
- 2 tablespoons lime juice
- 2 dessertspoons cornflour
- 6 dessertspoons blackstrap molasses, plus extra for drizzling

To decorate
- strawberries
- icing sugar

banoffee and quinoa custard pie

Pastry base

- 150 g (5 oz) rye flour
- 1 teaspoon linseed
- pinch of carob powder
- pinch of cinnamon
- 2 tablespoons rapeseed oil
- 50 ml (2 fl oz) soya milk
- 1 teaspoon brown sugar
- 1 teaspoon lime juice

Quinoa custard and coconut pouring cream

- 125 g (4 oz) quinoa seeds, flakes or flour
- 350 ml (12 fl oz) rice milk
- 475 ml (16 fl oz) soya milk
- 125 ml (4 fl oz) maple syrup
- 2 tablespoons sunflower oil
- 1 teaspoon instant decaffeinated coffee
- pinch of salt
- 1 tablespoon lemon juice
- 200 ml (7 fl oz) coconut milk
- 1 teaspoon vanilla essence
- 100 ml (3½ fl oz) rapeseed oil

Date toffee

- 50 g (2 oz) dates, finely chopped
- 175 ml (6 fl oz) soya milk
- 25 g (1 oz) coconut oil
- 2 teaspoons brown sugar
- 1 teaspoon blackstrap molasses
- 1 teaspoon lemon juice
- 2 bananas, sliced

1 Oil a 20 cm (8 inch) flan dish. Preheat the oven to 180°C (350°F), Gas Mark 4. Soak the dates for the toffee in the soya milk.

2 Mix together all the pastry ingredients, then roll out on a floured surface and use to line the prepared flan dish. Prick the pastry all over with a fork, then bake for 20–25 minutes until lightly browned. Set aside to cool.

3 Meanwhile, make the custard. Place the quinoa and rice milk in a small saucepan, bring to the boil, then simmer gently for 15 minutes. Add 375 ml (13 fl oz) of the soya milk and beat well with an electric mixer or hand-held blender. Simmer for another 5 minutes. Add the maple syrup, then divide the mixture equally between 2 bowls. To one add the sunflower oil, coffee, salt and 1 teaspoon of the lemon juice. Mix thoroughly until smooth.

4 To make the coconut pouring cream, heat the remaining soya milk and, while still beating, add the remaining lemon juice. Add this liquid to the quinoa mixture without coffee, then add the coconut milk, vanilla essence and rapeseed oil and beat until smooth.

5 Now make the date toffee. Melt the coconut oil (if necessary), then place in a food processor or liquidizer and add the dates, sugar and molasses and blend until smooth and creamy. Add the lemon juice and blend again. Spread the date toffee in the pastry case, then cover with a layer of sliced banana.

6 Spread the quinoa and coffee mixture on the top and chill for 2 hours. Serve cold with the coconut pouring cream, and a dusting of cocoa powder, if you wish.

chocolate chip cookies

- coconut oil, for greasing
- 125 g (4 oz) self-raising wholemeal flour or plain flour plus 1 teaspoon baking powder
- 50 g (2 oz) soft brown sugar
- 1 teaspoon cinnamon
- 4 teaspoons carob powder
- pinch of salt
- 50 g (2 oz) finely chopped dates
- 100 ml (3½ fl oz) sweetened soya milk
- 75 ml (3 fl oz) rapeseed oil
- 1 teaspoon vanilla essence
- 1 teaspoon finely grated orange rind
- 25 g (1 oz) dairy-free chocolate or carob, coarsely grated or chopped

Great for a snack at any time, these cookies also go well with ice cream. For a special treat, serve them with a bowl of Chocolate Sauce (see page 113) for dipping.

1 Line a baking sheet with baking parchment and grease with coconut oil. Preheat the oven to 180°C (350°F), Gas Mark 4.

2 Place the flour, sugar, cinnamon, carob powder, salt and dates in a bowl and mix well. Add the milk, oil and vanilla essence and beat with an electric mixer or fork. Stir in the orange rind and grated chocolate.

3 Place 12 dessertspoonfuls of the mixture on the prepared baking sheet and smooth the tops with a wet knife.

4 Bake the cookies for 10 minutes, then cool on a wire rack. Store in an airtight container until needed.

sticky pudding with quinoa coconut ice cream

preparation: 15 minutes, plus freezing
cooking: 1 hour
serves: 6

1 First make the ice cream. Place the quinoa and rice milk in a saucepan, bring to the boil, then simmer gently for 15 minutes. Add the soya milk and beat with an electric mixer or blender. Simmer for another 5 minutes. Add the agave syrup and coconut milk and beat again.

2 Still beating, add the rapeseed oil, then the vanilla essence and the lemon juice. Add the banana and beat until the mixture is smooth. Transfer the mixture to a shallow container with an airtight lid and freeze for 12 hours, stirring every hour or two with a fork to break up any ice crystals.

3 Now make the sticky pudding. Preheat the oven to 180°C (350°F) Gas Mark 4. Put the prunes and apple juice in a small saucepan and simmer for about 5 minutes, until soft. Add the orange juice, molasses and avocado oil and mix until smooth, using a hand-held mixer or blender.

4 Place the flour, soya milk, cinnamon, sugar, ginger, lemon juice and orange rind in a bowl and mix until smooth. Stir in the chopped coconut oil.

5 Place 1 dessertspoon of prune mixture in each of six 8 cm (3¼ inch) ovenproof ramekins and top with 2 dessertspoons of cake mixture. Cover each ramekin with a piece of oiled baking parchment and fasten in place with an elastic band. Place the ramekins in a deep roasting tin and pour in boiling water to reach about halfway up the dishes and bake for 35–40 minutes.

6 Run the blade of a sharp knife around the edge of each ramekin to loosen the puddings, then turn them out on to plates and decorate, if you wish, with slices of mango or peach. Serve with the ice cream.

Quinoa coconut ice cream
- 75 g (3 oz) quinoa seeds, flakes or flour
- 175 ml (6 fl oz) rice milk
- 175 ml (6 fl oz) soya milk
- 50 ml (2 fl oz) agave or maple syrup
- 200 ml (7 fl oz) coconut milk
- 100 ml (3½ fl oz) rapeseed oil
- 1 tablespoon lemon juice
- 1 teaspoon vanilla essence
- 1 banana, chopped

Sticky pudding
- 125 g (4 oz) ready-to-eat dried prunes
- 200 ml (7 fl oz) apple juice
- juice of 1 orange
- 2 tablespoons blackstrap molasses
- 1 tablespoon avocado oil
- 175 g (6 oz) self-raising flour
- 175 ml (6 fl oz) soya milk
- ½ teaspoon cinnamon
- 1 tablespoon soft brown sugar
- ½ teaspoon finely chopped fresh root ginger
- 1 dessertspoon lemon juice
- 1 teaspoon finely grated orange rind
- 50 g (2 oz) chilled and solidified coconut oil, chopped

index

index

acknowledgements

Executive Editor Nicola Hill

Executive Art Editor Joanna MacGregor

Designer Bill Mason

Special Photography Clive Bozzard-Hill

Picture Librarian Jennifer Veall

Production Controller Martin Croshaw

Photography **Octopus Publishing Group Limited**/Clive Bozzard-Hill 3, 5, 13, 19, 23, 27, 31, 35, 37, 39, 43, 45, 49, 53, 57, 61, 65, 69, 73, 77, 81, 85, 87, 89, 93, 97, 99, 103, 105, 107, 111, 115, 119, 123/Stephen Conroy 8 top left/William Reavell 7, 8 bottom right